Close Reading with Paired Texts

Level 1

Engaging Lessons to Improve Comprehension

Authors
Lori Oczkus, M.A.
Timothy Rasinski, Ph.D.

Shell Education

Digital Texts

To obtain digital copies of all the texts in this resource, scan the QR code or visit our website at **http://www.shelleducation.com/paired-texts/**.

Publishing Credits

Corinne Burton, M.A.Ed., *President*; Jodene Lynn Smith, M.A., *Contributing Author*; Emily R. Smith, M.A.Ed., *Content Director*; Jennifer Wilson, *Editor*; Courtney Patterson, *Multimedia Designer*; Monique Dominguez, *Production Artist;* Stephanie Bernard, *Assistant Editor*; Amber Goff, *Editorial Assistant*

Image Credits

pp. 7, 31, 48–49, 51, 80: iStock; all other images: Shutterstock

Standards

Shell Education
5301 Oceanus Drive
Huntington Beach, CA 92649-1030
http://www.shelleducation.com

ISBN 978-1-4258-1357-4

Table of Contents

About Close Reading

What Is Close Reading?

Students today need to carry a "tool kit" of effective reading strategies to help them comprehend a wide variety of texts. Close reading is one way for students to enhance their understanding especially as they read more challenging texts. The Common Core State Standards (2010) call for students to "read closely to determine what the text says explicitly and to make logical inferences from it and cite specific textual evidence when writing or speaking to support conclusions drawn from the text." Instead of skipping or glossing over difficult texts, students need to develop strategies for digging into the text on their own (Fisher and Frey 2012). Good readers dig deeper as they read and reread a text for a variety of important purposes. Close reading involves rereading to highlight, underline, reconsider points, ask and answer questions, consider author's purpose and word choice, develop appropriate oral expression and fluency, and discuss the text with others. In close reading lessons, students learn to exercise the discipline and concentration for analyzing the text at hand rather than heading off topic. Students of all ages can be taught to carefully reread challenging texts on their own for a variety of purposes.

Close reading involves rereading to highlight, underline, reconsider points, ask and answer questions, consider author's purpose and word choice, develop appropriate oral expression and fluency, and discuss the text with others.

Reciprocal Teaching, or the "Fab Four," and Close Reading

Reciprocal teaching is a scaffolded discussion technique that involves four of the most critical comprehension strategies that good readers employ to comprehend text—**predict**, **clarify**, **question**, and **summarize** (Oczkus 2010; Palincsar and Brown 1986). We refer to the reciprocal teaching strategies as "The Fab Four" (Oczkus 2012). These strategies may be discussed in any order but must all be included in every lesson. Together the four strategies form a powerful package that strengthens comprehension. Research has found that students who engage in reciprocal teaching show improvement in as little as 15 days (Palincsar and Brown 1986) by participating more eagerly in discussions. After just three to six months they may grow one to two years in their reading levels (Rosenshine and Meister 1994; Hattie 2008).

The reciprocal teaching strategies make it a practical lesson pattern for close readings. First, students briefly glance over a text to anticipate and predict the author's purpose, topic or theme, and text organization. As students read, they make note of words or phrases they want to clarify. During questioning, students reread to ask and answer questions and provide evidence from the text. Finally, students reread again to summarize and respond to the text. Quick partner and team cooperative discussions throughout the process increase students' comprehension and critical thinking. A strong teacher think-aloud component also pushes student thinking and provides students the modeling and support they need to learn to read challenging texts on their own. The four strategies become the tool kit students rely on as they read any text closely.

About Close Reading *(cont.)*

What Is Reading Fluency?

Fluency refers to the ability to read and understand the words encountered in texts accurately and automatically or effortlessly (Rasinski 2010). All readers come to a text with a limited or finite amount of cognitive resources. If they have to use too much of their cognitive resources to decode the words in the text, they have less of these resources available for the more important task in reading—comprehension. Readers who are not automatic in word recognition are easy to spot. They read text slowly and laboriously, often stopping at difficult words to figure them out. Although they may be able to accurately read the words, their comprehension suffers because too much of their attention had to be devoted to word recognition and away from comprehension. So although accuracy in word recognition is good, it is not enough. Fluency also includes automaticity. Good readers are fluent readers.

Fluency also has another component. It is prosody, or expressive reading. Fluent readers read orally with expression and phrasing that reflect and enhance the meaning of the passage (Rasinski 2010). Research has demonstrated that readers who are accurate, automatic, and expressive in their oral reading tend to be readers who read orally *and* silently with good comprehension. Moreover, students who perform poorly on tests of silent reading comprehension exhibit difficulties in one or more areas of reading fluency.

Fluency and Close Reading

How does a person become fluent? The simple answer is practice. However, there are various forms of practice in reading that nurture fluency in students. Students need to hear and talk about fluent reading from and with more proficient readers. In doing so, they develop an understanding of what actually constitutes fluent reading.

Fluency should be an essential part of close reading. Without some degree of fluency, it is difficult for students to successfully engage in close reading. If readers have to invest too much cognitive energy into the lower level-tasks of word recognition, they will have less energy available for the tasks required of close reading—interpreting author's purpose, noting detailed information, making inferences, etc. Close reading, by definition, requires readers to read a text more than once for different purposes. Reading a text more than once is called *repeated reading*. Moreover, one of the purposes for repeated reading can and should be to read a passage with a level of fluency that reflects the meaning of the text (Rasinski and Griffith 2010). For fluency strategies to use with students, see page 124.

By combining close reading using reciprocal teaching strategies with fluency, we end up with greater reading benefits for students than if close reading and fluency were taught and practiced separately. It is simply more efficient, more effective, and more authentic to deal with both of these critical competencies together. We call it *synergy*. Your students will call it *fun*!

About Close Reading (cont.)

Why Pair Fiction and Nonfiction Texts?

Standards point out that from the initial stages of literacy development, students need exposure to both fiction and nonfiction texts. Yet the previous conventional wisdom was to focus primarily on fiction and gradually move toward more nonfiction. We provide a balance of the two texts throughout this book. In doing so, we give students opportunities to explore and gain proficiency in close reading strategies with a range of text types.

When pairing texts, we also provide a content connection between them. One passage can help build background knowledge while the other passage focuses on building interest. Our paired texts allow students to engage in comparing and contrasting various types of texts, which in itself is a form of close reading.

The pairing of texts also helps students see that different forms of texts may require different levels or types of reading fluency. Fiction, including poetry, is written with voice. Authors and poets try to embed a voice in their writing that they wish the reader to hear. Texts written with voice should be read with expression. Thus, these texts lend themselves extremely well to reading with appropriate fluency. While nonfiction may also be written with voice, it is a different type of writing that often requires a different form of expression and fluency. By pairing these forms of texts, we offer students opportunities to master fluent reading in two forms.

Since multiple reading encounters with the same text are required in close reading activities, you will notice the texts are not very long. Students will be able to reread the engaging texts for multiple purposes to achieve greater success with their comprehension of the texts.

Close Reading and Differentiation

The close reading lessons in this resource are filled with many options for scaffolding to meet the needs of all students, including English language learners and struggling readers. The lessons offer a variety of stopping points where the teacher can choose to think aloud and provide specific modeling, coaching, and feedback. Understanding your students' background knowledge and interests will help you decide whether you should read the informational texts first or grab students' interests by starting with the fictional texts. Throughout the lessons, vocabulary is addressed in a variety of creative ways that will help students who struggle to better understand the text. Sentence frames, such as *I think I will learn _____ because_____* or *I didn't get the word _____, so I _____,* provide students with a focus for their rereading tasks and discussions with peers. Creative options for rereading the texts to build fluency and comprehension give students who need more support lots of meaningful practice.

About Close Reading *(cont)*

Effective Tips for Close Reading Lessons

To make the most out of close reading lessons, be sure to include the following:

1. **Text Focus**

   Throughout the lessons, keep the main focus on the text itself by examining how it is organized, the author's purpose, text evidence, and reasons why the author chose certain words or visuals.

2. **Think Alouds**

   Model close reading using teacher think alouds to help make thinking visible to students. For example, before asking students to find words to clarify, demonstrate by choosing a word from the text and showing different ways to clarify it.

3. **Cooperative Learning**

   Students' comprehension increases when they discuss the reading with others. Ask partners or groups to "turn and talk" during every step of the lesson.

4. **Scaffolding**

   Some students need extra support with comprehension or fluency. Use the suggestions on pages 123–124 that include sentence frames, ways to reread the text, props, gestures, and other ideas to reach every learner and make the lessons engaging.

5. **Metacognition/Independence**

   Name the rereading steps for students throughout the lessons. This will help them remember how to read closely when they encounter rigorous texts on their own. For example, before questioning say, "Now let's reread the text to find evidence as we ask and answer our questions."

Adapted from Lori D. Oczkus (2010)

A Close Reading Snapshot

Below is an example showing what one lesson might look like.

Students gather on the rug with clipboards, crayons, and copies of the poem "Planting, Waiting, Growing" by Katrina E. Housel. Mr. Jimenez projects a copy of the poem as students study the title and pair share predictions. Students read the poem and underline one word each that they already know and circle words that they want to learn. The class reads the poem multiple times, paying attention to the stanza breaks. In subsequent rereadings, pairs discuss the question frame *Why did the author use the word _____ to describe _____?* Partners sketch drawings to summarize the events in the poem.

Lesson Plan Overview

Teacher Pages

The lessons have overview pages that include summaries of the themes students will focus on and and answer keys. Each lesson includes two Teacher Notes charts, one for the nonfiction text and one for the fiction text. Both charts follow the same structure as below. **Note:** You will find some teacher modeling suggestions in the right hand columns of the charts. Prior to implementing the lessons, provide students with copies of the texts to mark throughout the lessons, and project larger versions of the texts for the class to see so that you can model important steps in the close-reading process. You can find digital copies of the texts at **http://www.shelleducation.com/paired-texts/**.

Lesson Steps	Purpose
Ready, Set, Predict!	In this section, students will: • skim the text • anticipate the topic • think about the author's purpose • think about text organization
Go!	In this section, students will: • read the text independently • anticipate the topic • think about the author's purpose • think about text organization • listen to the teacher read the text aloud • reread the text for various purposes • focus on various aspects of fluency
Reread to Clarify	In this section, students will: • work independently, in pairs, or in small groups to reread the text and identify words or phrases they want to clarify • use various clarifying strategies such as sounding out, studying word parts, visualizing content, and rereading
Reread to Question	In this section, students will: • work independently, in pairs, or in small groups to reread the text and ask and answer questions about the text • use text evidence to answer questions that are self-generated or asked by the teacher
Reread to Summarize and Respond	In this section, students will: • work independently, in pairs, or in small groups to reread the text and summarize the main ideas and details • evaluate the text • share text evidence to support their summaries of the text

Lesson Plan Overview *(cont.)*

Student Pages

After reading each pair of fiction and nonfiction texts, the lesson plan continues with opportunities for comparing the two texts and creative follow-up options that can be conducted with the whole class, small groups, partners, or as independent work in a center.

Response Pages

Each text has a follow-up activity page where students use their knowledge of the text to answer text-dependent questions.

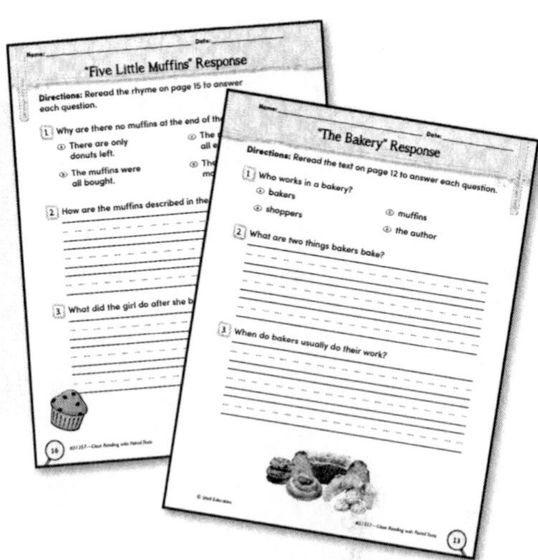
Name: Date:
"Five Little Muffins" Response
Directions: Reread the rhyme on page 15 to answer each question.
1 Why are there no muffins at the end of th
Ⓐ There are only donuts left.
Ⓑ The muffins were all bought.
2 How are the muffins described in the
3 What did the girl do after she b

Name: Date:
"The Bakery" Response
Directions: Reread the text on page 12 to answer each question.
1 Who works in a bakery?
Ⓐ bakers
Ⓑ shoppers
Ⓒ muffins
Ⓓ the author
2 What are two things bakers bake?
3 When do bakers usually do their work?

Comparing the Texts

This activity page offers creative reasons for students to reread both texts and synthesize information from both to accomplish a task. A few examples include: writing a news account, writing a poem, filling in a graphic organizer, or making a game.

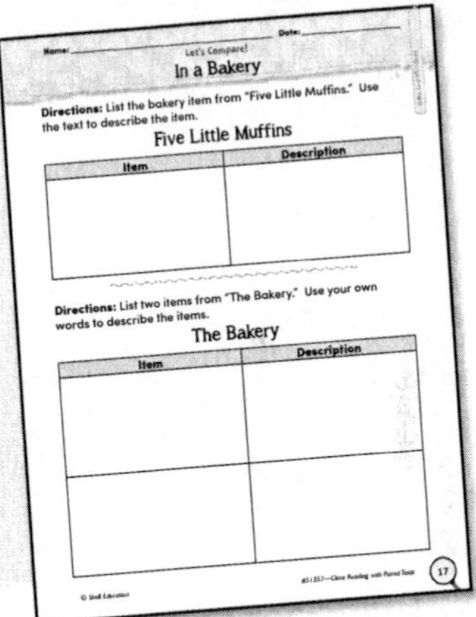
Name: Date:
Let's Compare!
In a Bakery
Directions: List the bakery item from "Five Little Muffins." Use the text to describe the item.
Five Little Muffins

Item	Description

Directions: List two items from "The Bakery." Use your own words to describe the items.
The Bakery

Item	Description

All About the Content

This activity page offers four activities that students can choose from that focus on their comprehension of the paired texts. The activities have the same focus in each lesson: reading, fluency, word study, and writing.

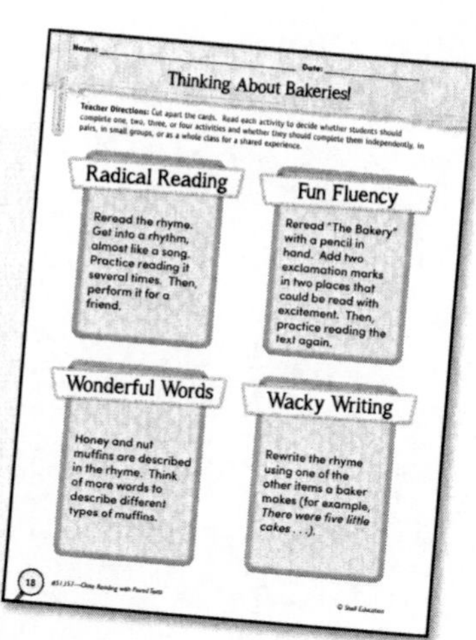
Name: Date:
Thinking About Bakeries!
Radical Reading
Reread the rhyme. Get into a rhythm, almost like a song. Practice reading it several times. Then, perform it for a friend.
Fun Fluency
Reread "The Bakery" with a pencil in hand. Add two exclamation marks in two places that could be read with excitement. Then, practice reading the text again.
Wonderful Words
Honey and nut muffins are described in the rhyme. Think of more words to describe different types of muffins.
Wacky Writing
Rewrite the rhyme using one of the other items a baker makes (for example, *There were five little cakes . . .*).

Unit 1 Overview

Bakeries

Theme Summary

A baker rises before the sun to get his job done, and what a yummy job it is . . . baking cakes, cookies, breads, and muffins! Students will read and respond to a cute rhyme about muffins and a nonfiction text about the job of a baker. This pair of texts is sure to make everyone hungry!

Answer Key

"The Bakery" Response (page 13)

1. A. bakers
2. Bakers bake muffins, cakes, bread, and cookies. (Accept any two.)
3. Bakers get up early to bake, so have everything ready before the store opens.

"Five Little Muffins" Response (page 16)

1. B. The muffins were all bought.
2. The muffins are the kind with the *honey and the nuts on the top*.
3. She *ran away*.

Let's Compare! In a Bakery (page 17)

Students should list the baked goods below in the charts. Check that the descriptions match the baked goods listed.

Five Little Muffins: muffins

The Bakery: cakes, bread, and cookies

Standards

- Use illustrations and details in a story to describe its characters, setting, or events.
- Describe the connection between two individuals, events, ideas, or pieces of information in a text.
- Read with sufficient accuracy and fluency to support comprehension.

Materials

- *The Bakery* (page 12)
- *"The Bakery" Response* (page 13)
- *Five Little Muffins* (page 15)
- *"Five Little Muffins" Response* (page 16)
- *Let's Compare! In a Bakery* (page 17)
- *Thinking About Bakeries!* (page 18)
- pencils
- index cards

Comparing the Texts

After students complete the lessons for each text, have them work in pairs or groups to reread both texts and complete the *Let's Compare! In a Bakery* activity page (page 17). Finally, students can work to complete the *Thinking About Bakeries!* matrix (page 18). The matrix activities allow students to work on the important literacy skills of reading, writing, vocabulary, and fluency. **Note:** Be sure to read each activity prior to implementation to see if it's intended for students to complete independently, in pairs, in small groups, or as a whole class for a shared experience. Make adjustments to the activities according to students' abilities.

Nonfiction Text Teacher Notes

The Bakery

	Lesson Steps	Teacher Think Alouds
Ready, Set, Predict!	• Distribute the text to students and display a larger version. Have them do a quick and quiet text walk to preview the text. Tell them to predict what the text will be about.	
Go!	• Read the text aloud to students once through without stopping. Model fluent reading. • Discuss reading fluency with students as you reread the text. Identify words that can be emphasized as they are read. Have students circle the words with pencils.	"Do you notice how I emphasize the word *must*? Emphasizing words keeps the reading interesting and helps with the meaning of the text, too."
Reread to Clarify	• Have students work with partners to reread the text to clarify. Have them underline words or sentences that are long, tricky, or fun to read. Have students answer question stems such as *The word _____ is tricky, so I _____* or *The sentence _____ is really long, so I _____.* • Tell students to discuss the tricky or confusing words or ideas and any strategies they used to clarify the words.	"The word *freshly* is tricky, so I look for parts I know. I figure out the word *fresh* and then add the *-ly* ending sound."
Reread to Question	• Write question prompts, such as *What words in the story support _____?* or *What does the author mean by _____?* on index cards. Tell students to reread the text to question. • Distribute an index card to each pair of students. Have pairs work together to reread the text and answer the questions. Have them switch cards with another pair and try to answer each others' questions. • Have students respond to the question and prompts on page 13.	
Reread to Summarize and Respond	• Ask students to reread the text to summarize. Have them share aloud anything they learned about bakeries from reading it. • Create a cause/effect graphic organizer to analyze the text with students. Provide causes for students if needed: *Bakers bake many treats* or *Bakers get up early to bake.*	"As I read, I think about what happens next. This connection is called *cause and effect*. I read that bakers bake many treats. I look for what happens next or after. This is the effect."

***Note:** For more tips, engagement strategies, and fluency options to include in this lesson, see pages 122–128.

Name:______________________ Date:______________

The Bakery

A bakery is filled with many yummy treats. Bakers make them for people to buy. They make bread and cakes. Many kinds of muffins are for sale, too. Bakers bake cookies in all shapes and sizes.

Bakers need many things to bake their goods. They need flour and sugar. They need salt and spices. Bakers use many eggs. They need butter and oil. Fruits and candies are often used in baking, too.

Bakers get up early to bake. They must have everything ready before the store opens. Shoppers rush in to buy the freshly baked treats.

Name: ______________________ Date: ______________

"The Bakery" Response

Directions: Reread the text on page 12 to answer each question.

1. Who works in a bakery?

   Ⓐ bakers
   Ⓑ shoppers
   Ⓒ muffins
   Ⓓ the author

2. What are two things bakers bake?

3. When do bakers usually do their work?

Fiction Text Teacher Notes

Five Little Muffins

	Lesson Steps	Teacher Think Alouds
Ready, Set, Predict!	• Provide the text to students and display a larger version. Ask them to preview the text and illustrations. Ask students to turn to partners and make predictions using the following prompt: *I think this text is about _____ because _____.* • Review the format of the text. Help students to note that the text repeats.	"I see the text repeats itself over and over again. Each time, the only thing that changes is the number until the final verse. This will help me when reading the text."
Go!	• Read the text aloud as students follow along. Model fluent reading. • Discuss with students how to read the text fluently to help convey meaning and interest. • Chorally read the text aloud together as a class.	"Watch how I read the words *ran away* quickly, as if the girl runs away quickly with the muffin."
Reread to Clarify	• Ask students to reread the text to clarify. Tell them to circle words that that are tricky. Have partners use strategies to clarify the confusing parts using the following: *The word _____ is tricky, so I _____.* • Have students practice reading the rhyme with partners. Partners can take turns reading verses until they get to the last verse, which can be read together.	"The part *Along came a child with a penny to pay* is confusing, so I reread the text and I notice that the girl went into a bakery and bought a muffin. I think the words *a penny to pay* mean that she uses the penny to buy the muffin."
Reread to Question	• Pair students to reread the rhyme to question. One student can read the rhyme. The other can reenact the rhyme. Use manipulatives, such as counters or paper muffins, in the reenactment. After each verse, have the student reading the rhyme ask the following questions about the muffins: *How many muffins were taken? How many muffins are left?* Then, have students switch roles. • Have students respond to the question and prompts on page 16.	
Reread to Summarize and Respond	• Tell students to reread the text to summarize. Have them write summaries in 20 words or less. You may wish to have students work in small groups to create a shared writing experience. Assist students in getting started with the stem: *Once upon a time, a little girl _____.* • Work together as a class to combine summaries into one great class summary.	

***Note:** For more tips, engagement strategies, and fluency options to include in this lesson, see pages 122–128.

Name: ______________________ Date: ______________

Five Little Muffins

Traditional

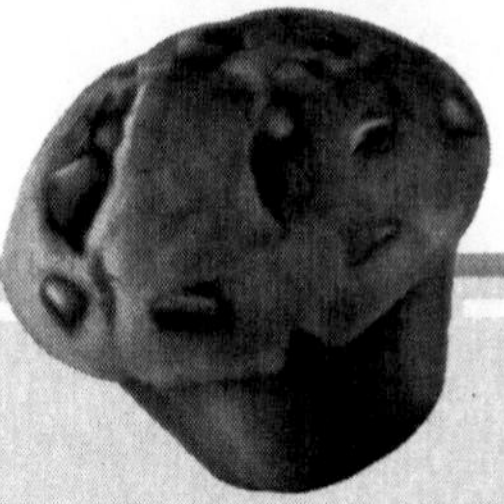

There were <u>five</u> little muffins in the bakery shop.
You know the kind with the honey and the nuts on the top.
Along came a child with a penny to pay.
She bought one muffin and ran away.

(Repeat the verse above counting down four, three, two, one. Then continue with the verse below.)

There were no little muffins in the bakery shop.
You know the kind with the honey and the nuts on the top.
Along came a child with a penny to pay.
She said, "WHAT? No muffins!" and ran away.

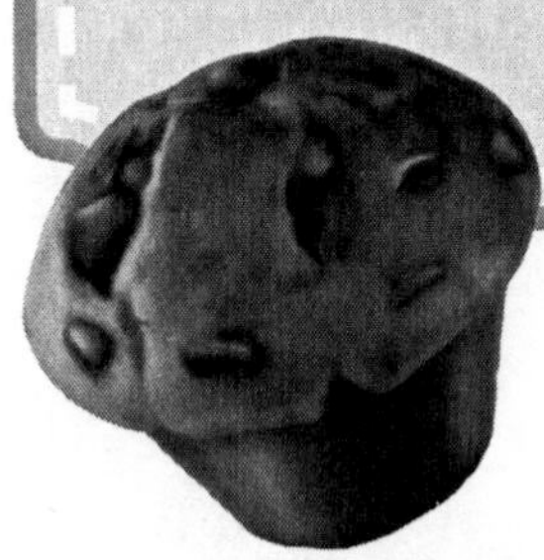

Name: ______________________ Date: ______________

"Five Little Muffins" Response

Directions: Reread the rhyme on page 15 to answer each question.

1. Why are there no muffins at the end of the rhyme?

   Ⓐ There are only donuts left.

   Ⓑ The muffins were all bought.

   Ⓒ The muffins were all eaten.

   Ⓓ The baker made more muffins.

2. How are the muffins described in the text?

3. What did the girl do after she bought a muffin?

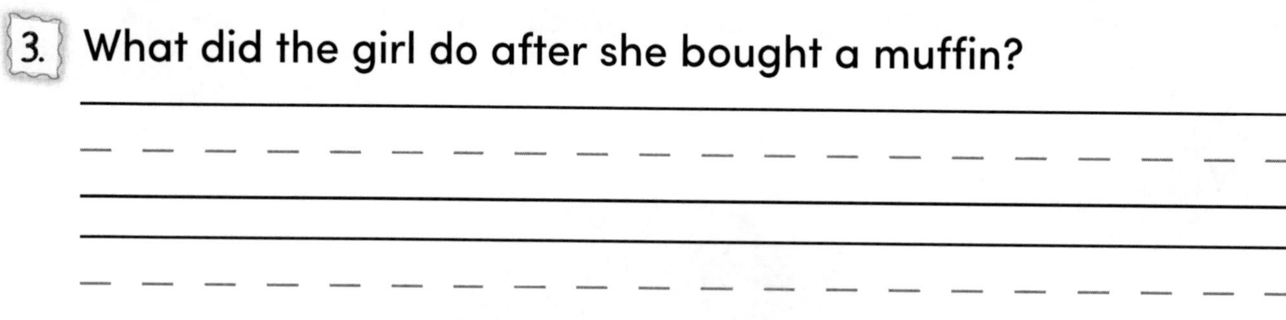

Name: ______________________ Date: ______________

Let's Compare!

In a Bakery

Directions: List the bakery item from "Five Little Muffins." Use the text to describe the item.

Five Little Muffins

Item	Description

Directions: List two items from "The Bakery." Use your own words to describe the items.

The Bakery

Item	Description

Name: ______________________________ Date: ______________

Thinking About Bakeries!

Teacher Directions: Cut apart the cards. Read each activity to decide whether students should complete one, two, three, or four activities and whether they should complete them independently, in pairs, in small groups, or as a whole class for a shared experience.

Radical Reading

Reread the rhyme. Get into a rhythm, almost like a song. Practice reading it several times. Then, perform it for a friend.

Fun Fluency

Reread "The Bakery" with a pencil in hand. Add two exclamation marks in two places that could be read with excitement. Then, practice reading the text again.

Wonderful Words

Honey and nut muffins are described in the rhyme. Think of more words to describe different types of muffins.

Wacky Writing

Rewrite the rhyme using one of the other items a baker makes (for example, *There were five little cakes . . .*).

Unit 2 Overview

Baseball

Theme Summary

Crack! A ball hitting a bat is a distinct sound. Get ready for a baseball game as students sing "Take Me Out to the Ball Game" and read a nonfiction text about the history of Little League®. Oh yeah, don't forget the peanuts!

Standards

- Identify who is telling the story at various points in a text.
- Distinguish between information provided by pictures or other illustrations and information provided by the words in a text.
- Use personal, possessive, and indefinite pronouns.

Materials

- *Play Ball!* (page 21)
- *"Play Ball!" Response* (page 22)
- *Take Me Out to the Ball Game* (page 24)
- *"Take Me Out to the Ball Game" Response* (page 25)
- *Let's Compare! Baseball Timelines* (page 26)
- *Thinking About Baseball!* (page 27)
- pencils
- crayons
- index cards
- drawing paper

Comparing the Texts

After students complete the lessons for each text, have them work in pairs or groups to reread both texts and complete the *Let's Compare! Baseball Timelines* activity page (page 26). Finally, students can work to complete the *Thinking About Baseball!* matrix (page 27). The matrix activities allow students to work on the important literacy skills of reading, writing, vocabulary, and fluency. **Note:** Be sure to read each activity prior to implementation to see if it's intended for students to complete independently, in pairs, in small groups, or as a whole class for a shared experience. Make adjustments to the activities according to students' abilities.

Answer Key

"Play Ball!" Response (page 22)

1. B. 1974
2. Answers will vary but may include: Kids learn *how to play baseball* or *how to be good sports*.
3. The text says, *At first, only boys could play in Little League®. Now, any child who wants to play baseball can join a Little League® team.*

"Take Me Out to the Ball Game" Response (page 25)

1. C. three
2. The text uses words such as *ball game* and *crowd*. This tells me that the setting is a crowded baseball game.
3. The author roots for the home team and thinks it is a shame if they don't win. This shows that the author likes the home team.

Let's Compare! Baseball Timelines (page 26)

Students should include the following on the timelines:

Take Me Out to the Ball Game

1st: Buy peanuts and cracker jack.

2nd: Three strikes, you're out!

Play Ball!

1939: Little League® begins.

1974: Girls join Little League®.

Nonfiction Text Teacher Notes

Play Ball!

	Lesson Steps	Teacher Think Alouds
Ready, Set, Predict!	• Provide students with the text and display a larger version. • Encourage students to quickly preview the text. Ask students to underline three tricky words in the text. You may also wish to have them work with partners to make predictions on what the text will be about.	"When I skim the text, I see a couple of words that I do not know the meanings of. I am going to pay close attention to those words as I read to try to figure out their meaning."
Go!	• Read the text aloud once through without stopping. Model fluent reading. • Discuss with students how reading fluently helps convey meaning and interest. • Have students work in pairs to practice reading the text with good fluency. Instruct them to focus on the rate in which they read the text, making sure to pause at appropriate places.	"Do you notice how I pause between each paragraph? How does the pause help you better understand the text?"
Reread to Clarify	• Ask students to reread the text to clarify by circling the three years listed and then underlining what events occurred in those years. Students can use three differently colored crayons to color code. • Discuss with students how using this color-coding strategy helps them clarify the information in the text.	"When I see many years listed in a text, it means many events happened. I have to find ways to keep each event separate so that I do not get them confused. Using different colors for each event helps me see what events happen and when."
Reread to Question	• Write question starters such as *Who* ______ and *When* ______ on index cards. Distribute an index card to each student pair. Work with students to reread the text to question. • After each paragraph, have partners take turns asking one another questions about the paragraph using their question starters. Then, work as a class to answer some of the questions students come up with. • Have students respond to the question and prompts on page 22.	
Reread to Summarize and Respond	• Distribute drawing paper to students. Divide students into groups of four. Assign each group member a paragraph (1–4). Ask students to reread their assigned parts to summarize. Have them draw summaries that describe their assigned parts. • Tell groups to combine their drawings and then share their summaries out loud.	

Name: ______________________ Date: ______________

Play Ball!

By Debra Housel

Kids love baseball. They want to play. That's why Little League® began in 1939. It let children have their own baseball teams.

Kids join Little League® teams to learn how to play baseball. They learn how to be good sports, too. They play against other teams.

At first, only boys could play in Little League®. In 1974, girls were allowed. Then, in 1990, the Challenger Division began. It is for kids with disabilities.

Today, there are thousands of Little League® teams. Any child who wants to play baseball can join a Little League® team.

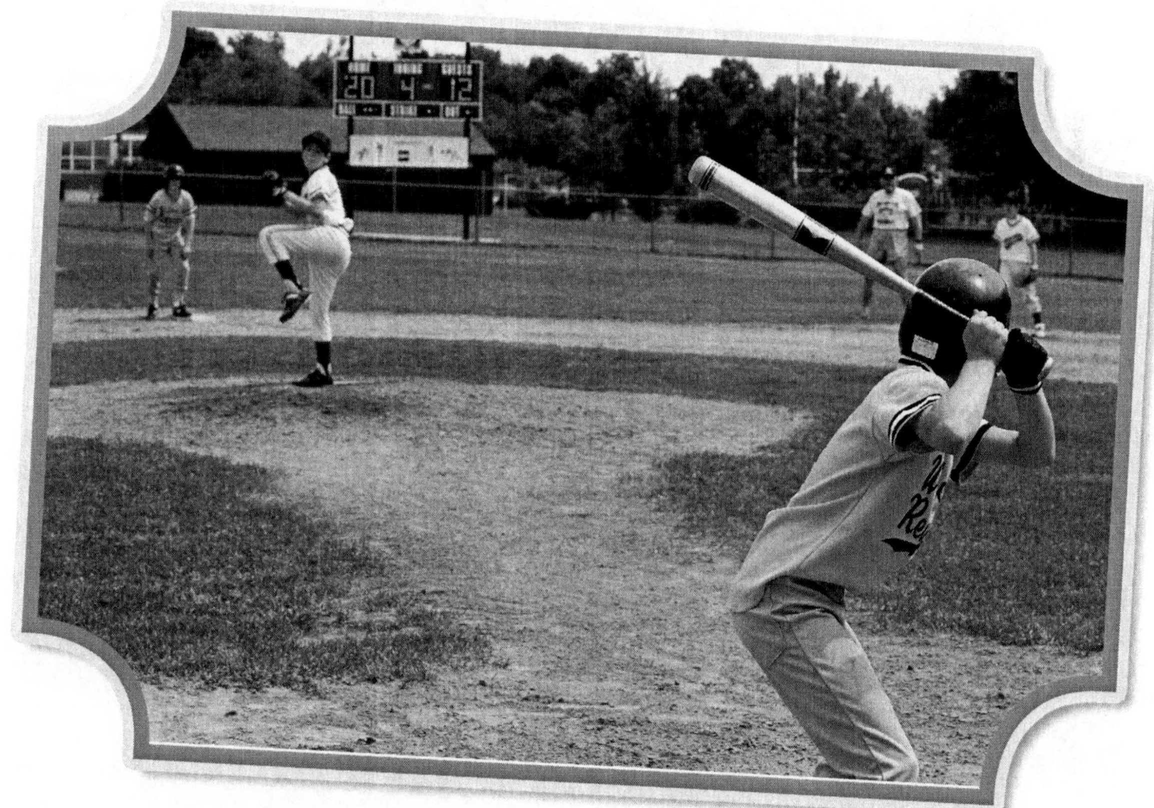

Name: ______________________ Date: ______________

"Play Ball!" Response

Directions: Reread the text on page 21 to answer each question.

1. When did girls join Little League®?

   Ⓐ 1939

   Ⓑ 1974

   Ⓒ 1990

   Ⓓ They cannot play on Little League® teams.

2. How does the author describe what kids can learn by playing on Little League® teams?

3. Use the text to tell how Little League® has changed.

Fiction Text Teacher Notes

Take Me Out to the Ball Game

	Lesson Steps	Teacher Think Alouds
Ready, Set, Predict!	• Provide the text to students and display a larger version. Read the title aloud. Ask students to share with partners anything they already know about the text. • Have students preview the song. Tell them to work with partners to predict the author's purpose in writing it using the following: *I think the author wrote this song to _____ because _____.*	
Go!	• Sing (or read) the text to students. Discuss with students that even though it is a song, the song tells a story. • Invite students to join in on a second reading of the text if they know the song. • Discuss with students how singing the text helps or hinders reading the text with fluency.	"I notice that as I sing 'Take Me Out to the Ball Game,' it tells a little story about going to a baseball game."
Reread to Clarify	• Divide students into seven groups. Distribute magnifying glasses (page 126) to students. Tell them that they are detectives and they need to reread the text to clarify. Have them use their magnifying glasses to look for the trickiest words or phrases in the text. Have students discuss their tricky words and phrases with other students in their groups using the following: *I think the word/ phrase _____ is tricky, so I _____.*	"I don't understand the words *cracker jack*, so I use other words to try to figure it out. The text says, *Buy me some peanuts and cracker jack*. This means he wants to eat snacks, so cracker jack must be some sort of snack."
Reread to Question	• Tell students to reread the text to question. Ask them to consider whose perspective the song is from: *Who is singing this song?* Discuss how they can figure out who is singing the song: *What pronouns can help you identify who is telling the story in the song?* Have students identify words that show who is telling the story. • Have students respond to the question and prompts on page 25.	"Pronouns can help me understand who is telling a story. I see the word *me* in this song. This helps me know it is not a character telling the story. It is the author."
Reread to Summarize and Respond	• Ask students to reread the text to summarize by drawing pictures of themselves at a ball game. Have students include details from the text as part of their illustrations. • Review the close reading strategies with students by singing the song on page 128.	

Name:______________________ Date:__________

Take Me Out to the Ball Game

By Jack Norworth

Take me out to the ball game,
Take me out with the crowd.
Buy me some peanuts and cracker jack,
I don't care if I never get back,
Let me root, root, root for the home team,
If they don't win it's a shame.
For it's one, two, three strikes, you're out,
At the old ball game.

Name: ______________________ Date: ______________

"Take Me Out to the Ball Game" Response

Directions: Reread the song on page 24 to answer each question.

1. How many strikes until an out?

   Ⓐ one
   Ⓑ two
   Ⓒ three
   Ⓓ until the team wins

2. What words tell about the setting?

3. How does the author feel about the home team?

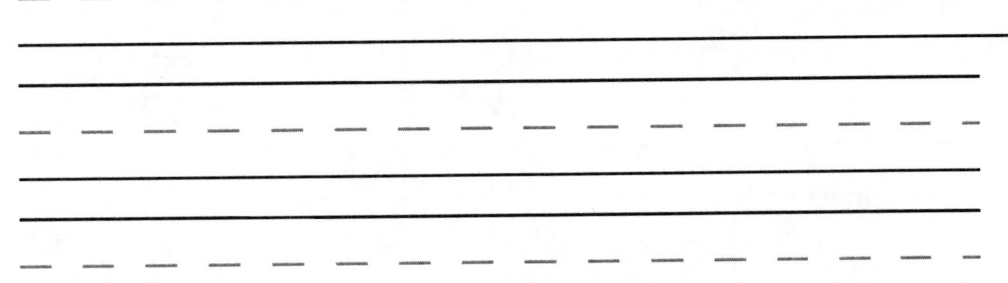

Name: ______________________ Date: ______________

Let's Compare!

Baseball Timelines

Directions: Reread both texts. Use the events below to complete the two timelines.

Nonfiction Events	Fiction Events
Little League® begins.	Buy peanuts and cracker jack.
Girls join Little League®.	Three strikes, you're out!

Take Me Out to the Ball Game

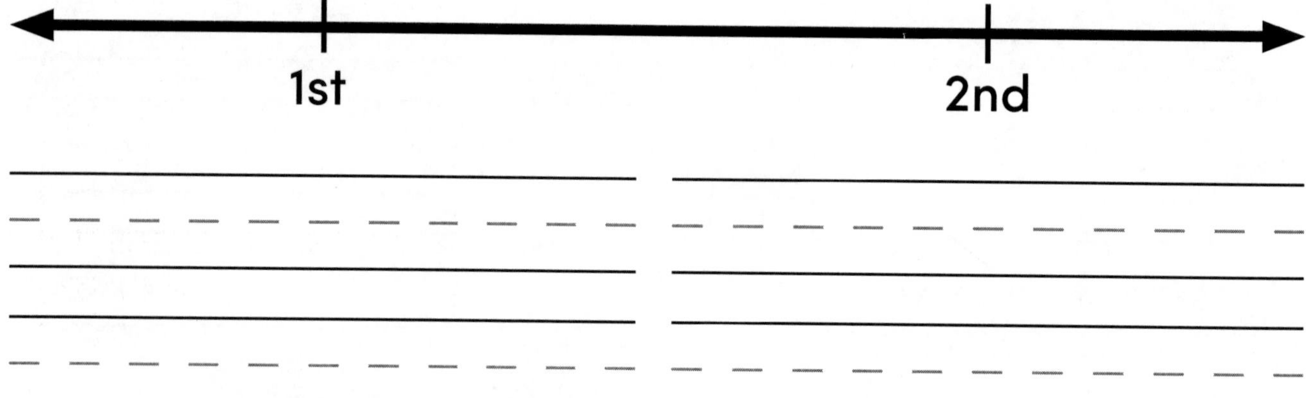

Play Ball!

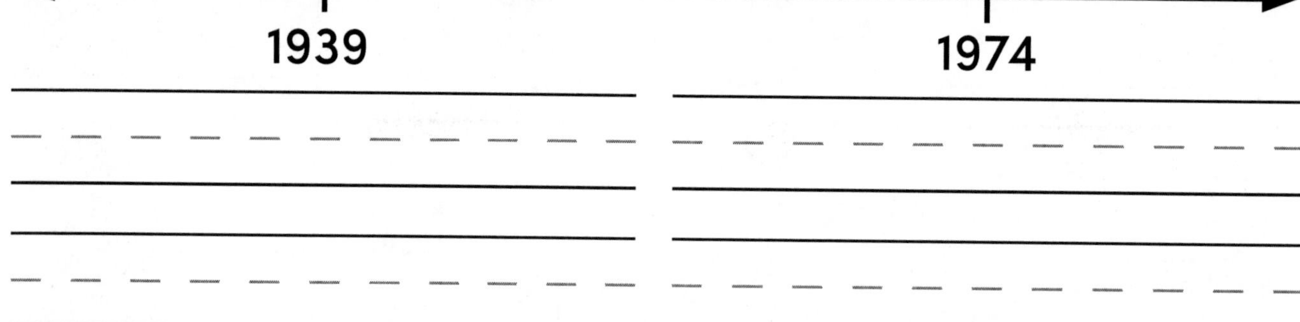

Thinking About Baseball!

Teacher Directions: Cut apart the cards. Read each activity to decide whether students should complete one, two, three, or four activities and whether they should complete them independently, in pairs, in small groups, or as a whole class for a shared experience.

Radical Reading

Practice reading or singing "Take Me Out to the Ball Game" several times until it sounds fluent. Then, digitally record yourself reading it. Play the recording for other students.

Fun Fluency

Practice singing "Take Me Out to the Ball Game" making your voice sound as if your team is winning. Practice it again as if your team is losing.

Wonderful Words

Write the word *baseball* in the middle of a sheet of paper. Draw a circle around the word. Around the circle, write as many words as you can think of about baseball.

Wacky Writing

Write about a time you were at a baseball game or watched one on television. Be sure to include a drawing.

Unit 3 Overview

Turtles

Theme Summary

What moves slowly and carries its home wherever it goes? You guessed it—a turtle. Students will enjoy this pair of texts about an animal that kids love. The fiction text is a reader's theater script about a lost pet and the nonfiction piece gives information about turtles. Come out of your shell and enjoy this text pair!

Answer Key

"All About Turtles" Response (page 31)

1. D. They can go inside their hard shells.
2. The text states that *many* turtles hibernate. This means that a lot of turtles hibernate but not all.
3. The author includes the details that turtles *do not have any teeth*, and they *use their beak-shaped mouths to tear their food.*

"Finding Tork" Response (page 34)

1. B. Winter is coming.
2. Kim's pet turtle is missing.
3. The author tells us that box turtles sleep all winter because it explains why Tork is hiding and sleeping.

Let's Compare! Hibernation (page 35)

Students' drawings will vary. Check that students' descriptions include some of the following from the texts: *Many turtles go to sleep; turtles save energy; Box turtles sleep in winter; They sleep all winter; He's sleeping.*

Standards

- Describe characters, settings, and major events in a story, using key details.
- Identify the main topic and retell key details of a text.
- Read words with inflectional endings.

Materials

- *All About Turtles* (page 30)
- *"All About Turtles" Response* (page 31)
- *Finding Tork* (page 33)
- *"Finding Tork" Response* (page 34)
- *Let's Compare! Hibernation* (page 35)
- *Thinking About Turtles!* (page 36)
- pencils
- crayons
- white drawing paper

Comparing the Texts

After students complete the lessons for each text, have them work in pairs or groups to reread both texts and complete the *Let's Compare! Hibernation* activity page (page 35). Finally, students can work to complete the *Thinking About Turtles!* matrix (page 36). The matrix activities allow students to work on the important literacy skills of reading, writing, vocabulary, and fluency. **Note:** Be sure to read each activity prior to implementation to see if it's intended for students to complete independently, in pairs, in small groups, or as a whole class for a shared experience. Make adjustments to the activities according to students' abilities.

Nonfiction Text Teacher Notes

All About Turtles

	Lesson Steps	Teacher Think Alouds
Ready, Set, Predict!	• Provide the text to students and display a larger version. Have them independently skim over the title and text. Ask students to predict what type of text it is (e.g., *article, directions, story*).	
Go!	• Read the text to students as they follow along. Model reading with expression by sounding excited at appropriate places. • Ask students to use yellow crayons to highlight the ending punctuation of each sentence in the text. • Discuss with students how the ending punctuation affects how you read the text.	"Notice how I make my voice sound excited when I read the sentence, *Now that's a good night's sleep!*"
Reread to Clarify	• Have students reread the text with partners to clarify. Ask them to be detectives and circle tricky or interesting words in the text that they want to know. Have small groups discuss any words that students circle. • Ask students to identify other words with inflectional endings. Have students underline the base words and circle the endings (e.g., *slow/ly* and *interest/ing*).	"The word *guessed* is tricky, so I look for parts I know. I figure out the word *guess* and then add the ending hyphen *-ed* to figure out the word."
Reread to Question	• Tell students that the title of a text is often the main idea of the text. Have students reread the title with you. Then, work together to reread to question. • As a class, reread each paragraph and then ask questions about it. Provide prompts, such as *How does a turtle eat?* and *When do turtles sleep?*, for partners to discuss. • Have students respond to the question and prompts on page 31.	"The text tells about how turtles protect themselves by pulling themselves into their shells. This detail tells more about the main topic. To help me remember this, I will ask a question about it. My question will be 'How do turtles protect themselves?'"
Reread to Summarize and Respond	• Tell students to reread the text to summarize by marking up the text using the following symbols: + main idea √ details # cool idea ☺ favorite part • Invite students to share their marked up papers with partners.	

***Note:** For more tips, engagement strategies, and fluency options to include in this lesson, see pages 122–128.

Name:______________________________ Date:______________

All About Turtles

What animal moves very slowly and carries its home wherever it goes? You guessed it—a turtle!

Turtles are known for their hard shells. A turtle can protect itself by pulling its head and legs inside the shell. This makes it hard for an enemy to get the turtle.

It is interesting to watch turtles eat. They do not have any teeth. Turtles use their beak-shaped mouths to tear their food.

When the weather gets cold, many turtles go to sleep. This is called hibernation. Hibernating helps turtles save energy. Do you know that some turtles hibernate eight months a year? Now that is a good night's sleep!

Name: ______________________________ **Date:** ____________________

"All About Turtles" Response

Directions: Reread the text on page 30 to answer each question.

1. Why is it hard for enemies to get turtles?

   Ⓐ They hibernate.

   Ⓑ They have beak-shaped mouths.

   Ⓒ They move slowly.

   Ⓓ They can go inside their hard shells.

2. Do all turtles hibernate? Which word in the text supports your answer?

   ____

3. The author states *it is interesting to watch turtles eat.* What details does the author include to support this?

   ____

Fiction Text Teacher Notes

Finding Tork

	Lesson Steps	Teacher Think Alouds
Ready, Set, Predict!	• Provide students with the text and display a larger version. Have students skim the text to determine the text structure. Then, discuss the format of the reader's theater script with students. • Ask students to make predictions using the following: *I think the author wrote this text in a reader's theater format because _____.*	"This text is not in a paragraph format. It is written like characters are talking to each other. The names of the characters are on the left. The words they say are on the right."
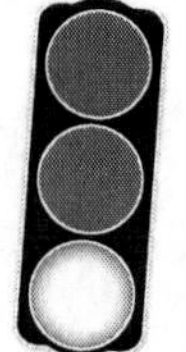 **Go!**	• Read the entire reader's theater script aloud. Model changing your voice slightly for each of the characters so that students get familiar with each of the parts.	"Do you notice I change my voice for Kim and Mom? Why do you think I do this? Does it help you in listening to my reading?"
 **Reread to Clarify**	• Have students reread the text in pairs to clarify. They should underline words or sentences they want to clarify. Have students discuss their circled parts and strategies they used to clarify them using the following: *The word _____ is tricky, so I _____.* • Explain what inflectional endings are. Ask students to underline the words with *-ing* endings (*missing, hiding, coming, sleeping*). Have them circle the *-ing* ending of each word.	"The word *sleeping* is tricky, so I look for parts I know. I figure out the word *sleep* and then add the *-ing* ending to figure out the word."
Reread to Question	• Tell students that good readers identify characters and settings as they read. Review the two characters in the script with students. Then, work together to reread the script to question. • Pair students, and have one student pick a character from the script to role-play and one student to be the interviewer. Have the interviewers hold up their fists to represent microphones as they ask their partners questions, such as *Why did you _____?* Then, students can switch roles. • Have students respond to the question and prompts on page 34.	
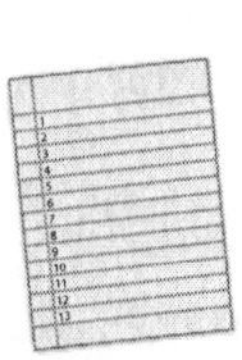 **Reread to Summarize and Respond**	• Tell students to reread the text to summarize. Have them think about the main points of the text. • Provide students with sheets of drawing paper. Ask them to draw pictures of the ending of the story. Then, have students show and explain their pictures to partners.	

Name: ______________________________ Date: ________________

Finding Tork

By Suzanne Barchers

Kim: Mom, can you help me find my turtle? He is missing. I have looked everywhere for him.

Mom: I think your turtle, Tork, is hiding.

Kim: Why?

Mom: Winter is coming. Box turtles sleep a lot in winter.

Kim: Why does Tork want to sleep?

Mom: Turtles slow down in winter. They sleep all winter.

Kim: Like bears?

Mom: Yes! We should look for quiet and cool places.

Kim: He is not under my bed.

Mom: Here he is. He's in the closet!

Kim: He's sleeping. When will he wake up?

Mom: He'll wake up when he's hungry!

Name: ______________________________ Date: ________________

"Finding Tork" Response

Directions: Reread the text on page 33 to answer each question.

1. Why does Mom think Tork is hiding?

   Ⓐ He is playing a game.

   Ⓑ Winter is coming.

   Ⓒ He is in the closet.

   Ⓓ He is not under the bed.

2. What problem does Kim face?

   ____

   ____

3. Why does the author tell us box turtles sleep all winter?

   ____

   ____

   ____

Name: ____________________ Date: ____________

Let's Compare!

Hibernation

Directions: Draw a picture of a turtle hibernating. Use both texts to write about what happens when turtles hibernate.

Thinking About Turtles!

Teacher Directions: Cut apart the cards. Read each activity to decide whether students should complete one, two, three, or four activities and whether they should complete them independently, in pairs, in small groups, or as a whole class for a shared experience.

Radical Reading

Practice reading the "Finding Tork" reader's theater script with a partner. Be sure to read it with lots of expression.

Fun Fluency

Practice reading "Finding Tork" by yourself. Use a different voice for each character. After you have practiced, perform your version for a friend.

Wonderful Words

Make a list of some of the quiet, cool places in your house where a turtle could hibernate.

Wacky Writing

Turtles can hide in their shells to protect themselves. Write about another animal you know and what it does to protect itself.

Unit 4 Overview

Time

Theme Summary

Tick, tock, tick, tock—our lives are run by the hands of the clock. This text pair provides unique ways for students to see time in everyday use. Students will learn what time a cobbler has to have the shoes ready by and know what time a train is leaving. All aboard!

Standards

- Retell stories, including key details, and demonstrate understanding of their central message or lesson.
- Know and use various text features to locate key facts or information in a text.
- Tell and write time in hours and half-hours using analog and digital clocks.

Materials

- *All Aboard* (page 39)
- *"All Aboard" Response* (page 40)
- *Cobbler, Cobbler* (page 42)
- *"Cobbler, Cobbler" Response* (page 43)
- *Let's Compare! A Busy Schedule* (page 44)
- *Thinking About Time!* (page 45)
- pencils
- paper
- instructional clock
- index cards

Comparing the Texts

After students complete the lessons for each text, have them work in pairs or groups to reread both texts and complete the *Let's Compare! A Busy Schedule* activity page (page 44). Finally, students can work to complete the *Thinking About Time!* matrix (page 45). The matrix activities allow students to work on the important literacy skills of reading, writing, vocabulary, and fluency. **Note:** Be sure to read each activity prior to implementation to see if it's intended for students to complete independently, in pairs, in small groups, or as a whole class for a shared experience. Make adjustments to the activities according to students' abilities.

Answer Key

"All Aboard" Response (page 40)

1. D. Kirk
2. There is a half an hour between each departing time.
3. Franklin's train departs at 3:00 P.M.

"Cobbler, Cobbler" Response (page 43)

1. B. half-past eight
2. Answers will vary. Students may include the words *mend my shoe* and *stitch* in their responses.
3. The picture helps the reader to visualize what a cobbler is. The picture shows a man working on a shoe.

Let's Compare! A Busy Schedule (page 44)

Students' drawings will vary. Check that the drawings represent the correct events.

Nonfiction Text Teacher Notes

All Aboard

	Lesson Steps	Teacher Think Alouds
Ready, Set, Predict!	• Read the title to students and have them predict what the text will be about. • Distribute the text to students and display a larger version. Point out the train schedule shown on the page. Discuss the layout of the train schedule and how to read it. Ask students to tell you why a train schedule might be important to someone.	
Go!	• Model reading the entire text to students, including reading the train schedule in sentence format. • Reread the text aloud with students. Chorally read the opening sentences. Echo read the information from the train schedule.	"I notice that the time 2:00 P.M. is directly across from Cypress Station in the train schedule. I read this as: *The train departs from Cypress Station at 2:00 P.M.*"
Reread to Clarify	• Tell students to be detectives and reread the text to uncover (circle) mysterious or confusing words that they want to know. Have them complete and share the following sentence frame with partners: *I do not know the word _____, so I _____.* • Pair students. Haave each partner find one word to share and tell two ways he or she figured it out.	
Reread to Question	• Ask students, "Do you think a sentence or a chart is easier to understand?" Allow time for discussion. • Write a sentence on the board to tell the departing time at each station (for example, *The train departs from Cypress Station at 2:00 P.M.*). Compare the layout of the train schedule with the sentence on the board. Discuss with students which is easier to gather information from. • Tell students to use the chart in the text to ask each other questions about the departing time at each train station: *Which station has a train departing at _____? What time does the train depart from _____ Station?* • Have students respond to the question and prompts on page 40.	
Reread to Summarize and Respond 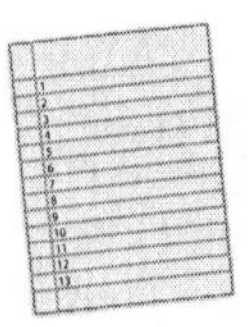	• Invite students to reread the text to summarize. • Provide students with sheets of paper. Have them re-create the train schedule from the text and add two more stops to the bottom of their new schedules.	"After reading the train schedule over and over, I see a pattern in the departing times column. I can continue the pattern as I add to the train schedule."

Name: ______________________ Date: ______________

All Aboard

Franklin is going to take a train. The trains leave every half hour. Franklin will get on at Katy Station. He will get off the train at Spring Station.

Station	Departing Time
Cypress Station	2:00 P.M.
Woods Station	2:30 P.M.
Katy Station	3:00 P.M.
Kirk Station	3:30 P.M.
Spring Station	4:00 P.M.

Name: ______________________ Date: ______________

"All Aboard" Response

Directions: Reread the text on page 39 to answer each question.

1. Which station has a train departing at 3:30 P.M.?

   Ⓐ Cypress
   Ⓑ Wood
   Ⓒ Katy
   Ⓓ Kirk

2. How much time is there between each train's departing time?

3. What time will Franklin's train leave?

Fiction Text Teacher Notes

Cobbler, Cobbler

	Lesson Steps	Teacher Think Alouds
Ready, Set, Predict!	• Briefly review telling time to the hour and half hour with students. Include using words such as: *two thirty,* as well as *half-past two.* • Provide the text to students and display a larger version. Read the title aloud to students and ask them to use the illustration to make predictions about what a cobbler is.	
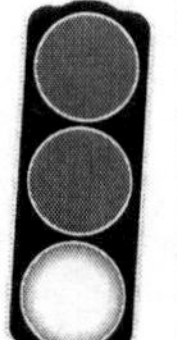 **Go!**	• Read the poem aloud to students. • Discuss the way you read the poem, including any emphasis you place on specific words. • Have the class chorally reread the poem several times. Encourage students to underline the emphasized words you discussed.	"Notice how I emphasize the word *much*. I want the listener to really pay attention to that word and know it is very late!"
Reread to Clarify	• Tell students to reread the poem to clarify. Ask them to circle the two times listed in the poem. • Discuss with students why the author may have included specific times in the poem and clarify how the times relate to the rest of the plot of the poem. • Model the times stated in the poem on an instructional clock. Use the text to help students clarify if the times listed in the poem are A.M. or P.M.	"When I read about times in a poem, I try to visualize what the clock looks like when it shows that time. I also think about whether it is day or night and what else might be going on at that time."
 **Reread to Question**	• Tell students to reread the poem to question. Provide students with index cards that have question stems, such as *Who* _____ and *When* _____, on them. Distribute one card to each student. • Divide the class into two lines to do a question switch. The first person in one line asks his or her question, and the first person in the other line tries to answer it. Then, students switch so that everyone gets to ask and answer questions. • Have students respond to the question and prompts on page 43.	
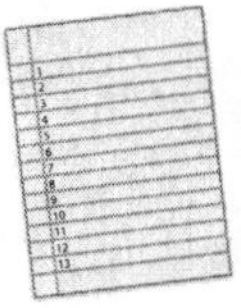 **Reread to Summarize and Respond**	• Reread the text with students to summarize. Make sure they understand the meaning of the poem and can summarize it in their own words. • Work together as a class to rewrite the poem. Do not worry if the poem rhymes, just get the meaning of the poem across in the retell. For example, *Shoemaker, shoemaker, fix my shoe. Get it done by 2:30 . . .*	"One of the ways I try to understand what is happening in a poem is by retelling it in my own words. This really shows I understand what is happening."

Name: ______________________________ Date: ________________

Cobbler, Cobbler

Traditional

Cobbler, cobbler, mend my shoe.
Get it done by half-past two.

No, half-past two is much too late,
So get it done by half-past eight.

Stitch it up and stitch it down.
Then I'll give you half a crown.

Name: ______________________ Date: ______________

"Cobbler, Cobbler" Response

Directions: Reread the poem on page 42 to answer each question.

1. What time does the narrator want his shoe fixed by?

   Ⓐ half-past ten
   Ⓑ half-past eight
   Ⓒ half-past one
   Ⓓ half-past four

2. Which words help you understand what a cobbler is?

3. How does the picture support the poem?

Name: ______________________________ Date: ______________

Let's Compare!

A Busy Schedule

Directions: Look at the events and times in the schedule. Then, draw each event.

The Cobbler's Day

Event	Time	Draw the Event
open the shop	7:30 A.M.	
fix shoes	10:00 A.M.	
have shoes ready	2:00 P.M.	
close the shop	4:00 P.M.	

Thinking About Time!

Teacher Directions: Cut apart the cards. Read each activity to decide whether students should complete one, two, three, or four activities and whether they should complete them independently, in pairs, in small groups, or as a whole class for a shared experience.

Radical Reading

Reread "Cobbler, Cobbler" as if you are in a very big hurry and need your shoe fixed.

Fun Fluency

Practice reading the train schedule in "All Aboard" in sentences using the voice of a train conductor. Use the following to help you: *The train departs from ______ Station at ______.*

Wonderful Words

Write the word *cobbler* in the center of a sheet of paper. Then, write words that describe a cobbler around the word.

Wacky Writing

Create a schedule of what you do each day starting with when you get up in the morning and ending with when you go to bed at night. Include the times for each event.

Unit 5 Overview

Collecting and Organizing Data

Theme Summary

Some people are more opinionated than others. This text pair encourages students to think about their favorite drinks. For the kids in the poem, it leads to a disagreement about which drink is best. The kids polled in the nonfiction text seem to find opinions about favorite drinks in a more mathematical way. Your students will enjoy forming their own opinions about this text pair!

Answer Key

"Favorite Drinks" Response (page 49)

1. C. bar
2. milk
3. Answers will vary. Students' questions should be answered with information from the graph.

"Molly, My Sister" Response (page 52)

1. B. argued
2. The characters are the narrator of the poem and her sister, Molly.
3. The characters cannot agree on the drink they love.

Let's Compare! Supporting Characters (page 53)

Students' graphs will vary. Check that they mark the graphs from the bottom up.

Standards

- With prompting and support, read prose and poetry of appropriate complexity for grade 1.
- Distinguish between information provided by pictures or other illustrations and information provided by the words in a text.
- Collect and represent information about objects or events in simple graphs.

Materials

- *Favorite Drinks* (page 48)
- *"Favorite Drinks" Response* (page 49)
- *Molly, My Sister* (page 51)
- *"Molly, My Sister" Response* (page 52)
- *Let's Compare! Supporting Characters* (page 53)
- *Thinking About Data!* (page 54)
- pencils
- crayons (particularly yellow)
- index cards

Comparing the Texts

After students complete the lessons for each text, have them work in pairs or groups to reread both texts and complete the *Let's Compare! Supporting Characters* activity page (page 53). Finally, students can work independently to complete the *Thinking About Data!* matrix (page 54). The matrix activities allow students to work on the important literacy skills of reading, writing, vocabulary, and fluency. **Note:** Be sure to read each activity prior to implementation to see if it's intended for students to complete independently, in pairs, in small groups, or as a whole class for a shared experience. Make adjustments to the activities according to students' abilities.

Nonfiction Text Teacher Notes

Favorite Drinks

	Lesson Steps	Teacher Think Alouds
Ready, Set, Predict!	• Provide the text to students and display a larger version. • Ask students to describe the layout of the page. Point out the graph as an additional text feature on this page. Ask students to predict how the graph will support the text.	"I quickly look at a page before I start to read it. I look for any text features that I can use to help me understand what I am reading. I notice a graph on this page. I think about how the graph can help me understand as I read."
Go!	• Read the text aloud to students. Review how to read the graph by pointing to the shaded areas of the graph and counting how many kids chose each type of drink. • Pair students and have them practice putting the information from the graph into sentences.	"When I see a graph, I can put the information from the graph into sentences as I think about the text. I say the information in the graph in order from left to right. For example, *Three kids chose milk.*"
Reread to Clarify	• Reread the text with students to clarify. Point out that the text tells that the most students chose sports drinks. Discuss how the graph helps clarify Collin's poll and the rest of the results.	
Reread to Question	• Discuss with the class how additional text features can support the text using the following questions: *What does the reader learn in the text that is not in the graph? What does the reader learn in the graph that is not in the text?* • Encourage students to reread the text and generate their own questions from either the text or the graph. Have them share their questions aloud with the class. • Have students respond to the question and prompts on page 49.	"Graphs can help readers better understand information. When I look at the graph, I ask myself, 'Which drink has the most votes?'"
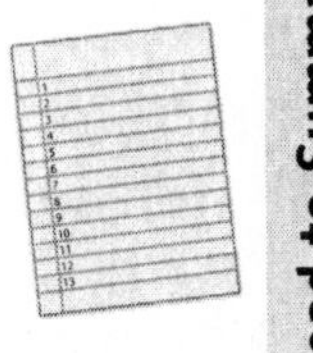 **Reread to Summarize and Respond**	• Reread the text with students to summarize by identifying which drink is chosen by the most kids and which drink is chosen by the least kids. • Organize the students into a living bar graph by having them line up in lines according to their favorite drinks. • Identify which drink is chosen by the most and the least students.	"When I read about kids choosing their favorite drink, I make a connection to the text by thinking about which drink I would choose."

***Note:** For more tips, engagement strategies, and fluency options to include in this lesson, see pages 122–128.

Name: ______________________________ Date: ______________

Favorite Drinks

Collin took a poll for his class. He asked the kids to name their favorite drinks. He found out that sports drinks were the drink chosen by the most kids. Collin decided to make a bar graph to show what he found. Below is the chart that he made.

Favorite Drinks

7		X			
6		X			
5		X			X
4		X		X	X
3	X	X		X	X
2	X	X	X	X	X
1	X	X	X	X	X
	milk	sports drinks	water	chocolate milk	lemonade

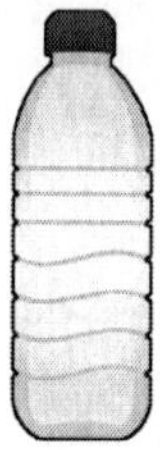

Name: ________________________ Date: ______________

"Favorite Drinks" Response

Directions: Reread the text on page 48 to answer each question.

1. What kind of graph did Collin make?

   Ⓐ tally
   Ⓑ poll
   Ⓒ bar
   Ⓓ chart

2. Which drink only has three votes?

   ____

3. Write a question that can be answered using the graph.

   ____

   ____

   ____

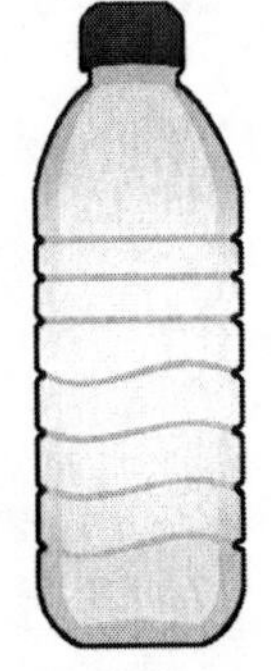

Fiction Text Teacher Notes

Molly, My Sister

	Lesson Steps	Teacher Think Alouds
Ready, Set, Predict!	• Provide the text to students and display a larger version. Have them turn to partners to describe the illustrations. • Ask students to predict the author's purpose with the following: *I think the author wrote this text to* _____ (e.g., *inform, persuade, entertain*) *because* _____.	
Go!	• Read the poem aloud to students as they follow along. Model fluent reading. • Have students highlight the punctuation in the poem with yellow crayons. Review with students how commas and question marks affect how the poem is read aloud.	"Listen to how I pause when I see the commas as I read. Listen to how my voice goes higher at the end of the sentence with a question mark."
Reread to Clarify	• Tell students to reread the text to clarify. Draw students' attention to the line, *And that was the reason we couldn't agree*. Help them clarify the sentence by explaining that the word *that* shows a transition from the previous sentence. • Have students reread the text and underline what happens before the word *that*. Invite partners to discuss the following: *Now that I have read the sentences, the word* that *stands for* _____.	"When I see the word *that* in the sentence, I know I need to understand what happened before to fully understand why the girls couldn't agree. I am going to go back and read what happens before this sentence. Rereading helps me clarify what I don't understand."
Reread to Question	• Provide each student with an index card with the word *character*, *setting*, or *plot* on it. Have students write questions about the story elements on their cards. For example, a student with the word *character* written on his or her card would write a question about the characters in the poem on the back of the card. Collect the cards. • Divide students into two teams. Ask the questions on the cards and have teams provide the answers. • Have students respond to the question and prompts on page 52.	"Here are some ways you can start your questions: *Who* _____*?, What* _____*?, Where* _____*?, When* _____*?, and Why* _____*?* If my card is *plot,* I want to know why the sisters are not agreeing, so my question is, 'What is different about each sister?' Asking this helps me remember that one sister likes coffee, and the other sister likes tea."
Reread to Summarize and Respond	• Tell students to reread the text to summarize by verbally telling partners two to three sentences explaining the plot of the poem. Support students in getting started with the words, *"Once upon a time there were two children . . ."*	"The poem is about two sisters that have a disagreement. One sister loves coffee, and one sister loves tea. Because of this, they cannot agree."

Molly, My Sister

Traditional

Molly, my sister,
And I fell out,
And what do you think
It was all about?

She loved coffee
And I loved tea,
And that was the reason
We couldn't agree.

Name: ______________________ Date: ______________

"Molly, My Sister" Response

Directions: Reread the poem on page 51 to answer each question.

1. What do the words *fell out* mean in this rhyme?

   Ⓐ fell down
   Ⓑ argued
   Ⓒ went outside
   Ⓓ got a drink

2. Who are the characters in this poem, and what is their relationship?

3. What is the problem in the poem?

Name: ______________________ Date: ______________

Let's Compare!

Supporting Characters

Directions: Ask classmates which character in "Molly, My Sister" they support.

Who Is Right?

6		
5		
4		
3		
2		
1		
	Support Molly	**Support Molly's Sister**

Directions: Write a sentence about the winner from the chart.

Thinking About Data!

Teacher Directions: Cut apart the cards. Read each activity to decide whether students should complete one, two, three, or four activities and whether they should complete them independently, in pairs, in small groups, or as a whole class for a shared experience.

Radical Reading

Reread "Molly, My Sister." Find words that rhyme in the poem. Name three other words that rhyme with the rhyming words you found.

Fun Fluency

Practice reading the poem with a partner. One partner should read the first two lines of each stanza. The other partner should read the last two lines of each stanza. Practice until the poem sounds the way you want it.

Wonderful Words

The word *poll* from the nonfiction text sounds the same as the word *pole*. Write a sentence using the word *poll*. Write another sentence using the word *pole*.

Wacky Writing

Favorite drinks are just the beginning! What are other favorites you have? Create a list of five more questions you want to poll your friends about.

Unit 6 Overview

Fractions

Theme Summary

Pies are easy to make and delicious to eat. Start cutting them to share and you have fractions. In this pair of texts, students will learn about the whole pie Jack Horner ate in the nursery rhyme and how to share equal pieces of pie in the nonfiction text. *Divide* students' time between these two texts and they will have a *whole* understanding of fractions!

Standards

- Describe characters, settings, and major events in a story.
- Use illustrations and details in a text to describe its key ideas.
- Partition circles and rectangles into two and four equal shares.
- Understand the concept of a unit and its subdivision into equal parts.

Materials

- *Pie Sharing* (page 57)
- *"Pie Sharing" Response* (page 58)
- *Little Jack Horner* (page 60)
- *"Little Jack Horner" Response* (page 61)
- *Let's Compare! Sharing Food* (page 62)
- *Thinking About Fractions!* (page 63)
- pencils
- index cards

Comparing the Texts

After students complete the lessons for each text, have them work in pairs or groups to reread both texts and complete the *Let's Compare! Sharing Food* activity page (page 62). Finally, students can work to complete the *Thinking About Fractions!* matrix (page 63). The matrix activities allow students to work on the important literacy skills of reading, writing, vocabulary, and fluency. **Note:** Be sure to read each activity prior to implementation to see if it's intended for students to complete independently, in pairs, in small groups, or as a whole class for a shared experience. Make adjustments to the activities according to students' abilities.

Answer Key

"Pie Sharing" Response (page 58)

1. C. pie cut in fourths
2. The top pie has the largest pieces because it is only cut into two pieces. Fewer people will need to share the whole pie.
3. If three people were to share a pie, the middle pie would be best because it is cut into three pieces.

"Little Jack Horner" Response (page 61)

1. C. a plum
2. The poem says that Jack is sitting in a corner *eating his Christmas pie*. This means that it is set in a house during Christmas.
3. There are no other characters named in the poem. Jack has a whole pie in the illustration.

Let's Compare! Sharing Food (page 62)

Students' drawings will vary. Check that the food items are split into the correct amounts in each box.

Nonfiction Text Teacher Notes

Pie Sharing

	Lesson Steps	Teacher Think Alouds
Ready, Set, Predict!	• Provide students with the text and display a larger version. • Allow time for students to skim the text and make predictions using the following: *I think that I will enjoy reading this text because _____.*	
Go!	• Read the text aloud to students. Then, point out the similar sentence structure within each section. • Divide students into three groups. Assign each group one section of the text. Read the first paragraph aloud. Then, have the groups read their assigned parts aloud.	"I see that the sentence structure is repeated in this text. This helps me as I read the text, and it helps me to better understand the math concept."
Reread to Clarify	• Help students reread the text to clarify. Have them circle the numbers in the text. Discuss the relationship between the number of pieces and the number of people who can share the pie. • Ask students to identify how the illustrations help clarify the information in the text: *I see _____ pieces of pie and the text tells me that _____ people can share the pie.*	"When I see illustrations on a page, I look closely to see how they can help me understand the text. I see a pie that is cut into two pieces. The text tells me this pie can be shared with two people. The illustration helps me see how the pie can be shared with two people."
Reread to Question	• Write questions about the fractions on index cards. (e.g., *How many people can share a pie divided into _____ pieces? What is the fraction for _____ out of _____ pieces of pie?*) Reread the text with students to question. Then, read the questions aloud, and have students answer them with partners. • Have students respond to the question and prompts on page 58.	
Reread to Summarize and Respond	• Tell students to reread the text to summarize. • Pair students to discuss other types of food that can be cut into pieces and shared the same way pie can be shared. • Review the close reading strategies with students by singing the song on page 128.	"After I have read a text, I think about ways I can use the information I have learned. This text makes me think that cake can be shared this way, too!"

***Note:** For more tips, engagement strategies, and fluency options to include in this lesson, see pages 122–128.

Name: ______________________ Date: ______________

Pie Sharing

Pies are fun to make and delicious to eat. It is fun to share pies with friends. Here are some different ways to share a pie.

This pie is cut into 2 equal parts. It can be shared by 2 people. Each person would get 1 of the 2 parts, or $\frac{1}{2}$.

This pie is cut into 3 equal parts. It can be shared by 3 people. Each person would get 1 of the 3 parts, or $\frac{1}{3}$.

This pie is cut into 4 equal parts. It can be shared by 4 people. Each person would get 1 of the 4 parts, or $\frac{1}{4}$.

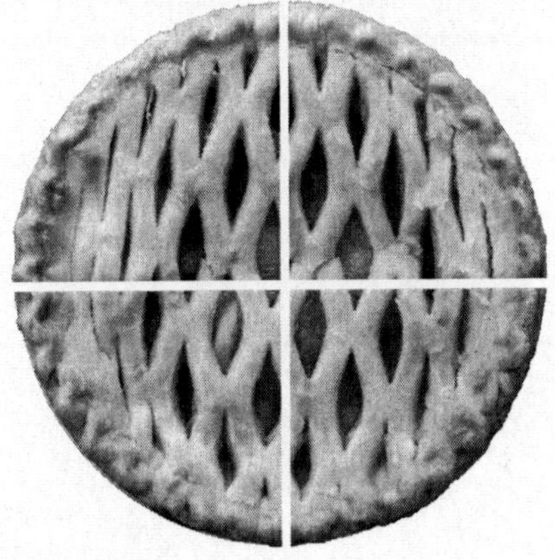

Name: ______________________________ Date: ______________

"Pie Sharing" Response

Directions: Reread the text on page 57 to answer each question.

1. Which pie can be shared by the most people?

   Ⓐ pie cut in half
   Ⓑ pie cut in thirds
   Ⓒ pie cut in fourths
   Ⓓ none of them

2. Why does the pie at the top have the largest pieces?

   ____

   ____

   ____

   ____

3. Which pie would you choose if you and two friends were going to share it?

   ____

   ____

Fiction Text Teacher Notes

Little Jack Horner

	Lesson Steps	Teacher Think Alouds
Ready, Set, Predict!	• Provide students with the poem and display a larger version. • Have students work with partners to make predictions about the character based on what they see in the illustration.	
Go!	• Chorally read the poem with students. • Ask students to work with partners to discuss the character they see in the illustration now that they have read the poem. • Discuss with students how their ideas about the character have been confirmed, changed, or been made more clear now that they have heard the poem.	"When I read a poem, I think about the characters. Knowing who is in the poem helps me better understand what happens in the poem."
Reread to Clarify	• Explain to students that there may be words in the poem that they do not know. • Have students reread the text with partners or in small groups to clarify. Ask them to underline words or sentences they want to clarify. Then, have them discuss the strategies they use to clarify their underlined parts.	"I am not sure how to read the word *thumb*. When I sound it out, I keep saying the /b/ sound. So I look at the illustration and see the boy has his thumb sticking up. This helps me know that the word is *thumb*."
Reread to Question	• Put students into small groups. Assign each group a question such as *Where is Jack sitting? Which words have quotation marks around them? What word in the poem rhymes with* plum? Tell groups to reread the text with their assigned questions in mind. • Proivde time for groups to discuss the answers to their questions. Then, have a discussion with the whole class. • Have students respond to the question and prompts on page 61.	
Reread to Summarize and Respond	• Ask students to work with partners to reread the poem, line by line, to summarize. Have them circle the words that are shown in the illustration. • Have students compare their findings with others. They can make changes to their papers, if needed.	

***Note:** For more tips, engagement strategies, and fluency options to include in this lesson, see pages 122–128.

Name: ____________________ Date: ____________

Little Jack Horner

Traditional

Little Jack Horner
Sat in a corner
Eating his Christmas pie.

He put in his thumb
And pulled out a plum
And said, "What a good boy am I."

Name: ______________________ Date: ______________

"Little Jack Horner" Response

Directions: Reread the poem on page 60 to answer each question.

1. What does Jack pull out of the pie?

   Ⓐ an apple
   Ⓑ an orange
   Ⓒ a plum
   Ⓓ the text does not tell

2. What does the poem tell you about the setting?

   ____

   ____

   ____

3. What evidence is there that Jack does not share his pie?

   ____

   ____

   ____

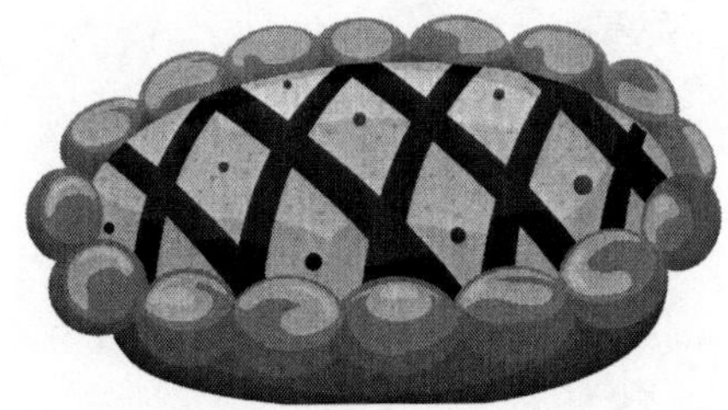

Name: ______________________________ Date: ____________________

Let's Compare!

Sharing Food

Directions: Choose a food item. Follow the directions in each box.

Draw a picture of a food item.	Draw a picture of the food. Divide it into 2 equal shares.
Draw a picture of the food. Divide it into 3 equal shares.	Draw a picture of the food. Divide it into 4 equal shares.

Thinking About Fractions!

Teacher Directions: Cut apart the cards. Read each activity to decide whether students should complete one, two, three, or four activities and whether they should complete them independently, in pairs, in small groups, or as a whole class for a shared experience.

Radical Reading

Choose either "Little Jack Horner" or "Pie Sharing." Practice reading the text until you can read it fluently. Record yourself reading it. Play the recording for a parent.

Fun Fluency

Reread either text with a hungry voice. Then, reread it with a stuffed voice. Which way sounds better?

Wonderful Words

Blueberry, *strawberry*, and *peach* are words that describe pies. Think of five other words that can describe pie. They do not have to be fruits!

Wacky Writing

Little Jack Horner was eating a Christmas pie. Choose your favorite holiday. Write about what foods your family likes to eat on that day.

Unit 7 Overview

Plants

Theme Summary

How does it happen? Put a seed in soil and add water. Wait patiently and something amazing will happen—a plant will grow! Keep watching and the plant grows larger. It may even get a flower or better yet, you may even get to eat part of the plant! In this pair of texts, students explore how plants grow and what they need to grow.

Answer Key

"How Plants Grow" Response (page 67)

1. B. The roots grow down in the soil.
2. The author uses *ground* and *soil* instead of *dirt*.
3. Leaves grow on the stem.

"Planting, Waiting, Growing" Response (page 70)

1. B. sharing the extra fruits and vegetables
2. Answers will vary. Check to see students describe a garden or an outdoor setting which may include dirt, sun, and plants.
3. The author likes gardening. She uses words like *fun* and *joy* in the poem.

Let's Compare! Plants' Needs (page 71)

Students should include at least one line for each box:

Planting, Waiting, Growing

soil/ground: *Dig a hole in the ground/ And put seeds all around;* **water:** *Give water to the shoots/To help them grow their roots;* **sun:** *Let the plants have some sun.*

How Plants Grow

soil/ground: *First there is a seed. It is under the ground;* **water:** *The roots get food and water for the plants.* **sun:** *The leaves need the sun to make food for the plant.*

Standards

- Ask and answer questions about key details in a text.
- Identify words and phrases in stories or poems that suggest feelings or appeal to the senses.
- Know the basic needs of plants and animals.

Materials

- *How Plants Grow* (page 66)
- *"How Plants Grow" Response* (page 67)
- *Planting, Waiting, Growing* (page 69)
- *"Planting, Waiting, Growing" Response* (page 70)
- *Let's Compare! Plants' Needs* (page 71)
- *Thinking About Plants!* (page 72)
- pencils
- drawing paper
- crayons (particularly yellow)

Comparing the Texts

After students complete the lessons for each text, have them work in pairs or groups to reread both texts and complete the *Let's Compare! Plants' Needs* activity page (page 71). Finally, students can work to complete the *Thinking About Plants!* matrix (page 72). The matrix activities allow students to work on the important literacy skills of reading, writing, vocabulary, and fluency. **Note:** Be sure to read each activity prior to implementation to see if it's intended for students to complete independently, in pairs, in small groups, or as a whole class for a shared experience. Make adjustments to the activities according to students' abilities.

How Plants Grow

	Lesson Steps	Teacher Think Alouds
Ready, Set, Predict!	• Provide the text to students and display a larger version. Ask them to do a text walk and make predictions about the text. • Have students pair-share their responses to the question, *What do you think the author's purpose is* (e.g., *to persuade, entertain, inform*)*?*	"I answer questions in complete sentences and provide reasons for my thinking. For example, 'I think the author wrote this to inform because it is in paragraph form.'"
Go!	• Read the text aloud as students follow along. • Discuss how the punctuation helps the reader know how to read the text. Ask students to pay close attention to the punctuation as they reread the text with partners.	
Reread to Clarify	• Have students reread the text to clarify. Tell them to circle words they want to clarify. Discuss ways students can figure out the meanings of any words they circle. • List the plant parts that are named in the text. Have students underline the sentences that clarify the plant parts' functions.	"I read in the text that one plant part is the roots. I read in the next sentence that *the roots get food and water for the plant*. This sentence helps me better understand what roots are."
Reread to Question	• Ask students to consider how the text is organized. Help students list the words that show how this text is organized in a sequence (i.e., *first*, *next*, and *then*). Pair students. Have them reread the text to question. Tell them to ask each other questions about how the text is organized. Provide stems such as: *What happens after _____?* and *What is the first _____?* to assist students. • Have students respond to the question and prompts on page 67.	"I notice the text is organized in the same way that a plant grows. The roots grow first, so they are named first in the text."
Reread to Summarize and Respond	• Provide students with sheets of paper. Have them reread the text to summarize by drawing diagrams of plants with the parts named in the text. Depending on students' abilities, ask them to include the functions next to the labels. Have students explain their diagrams to partners. • Review the close reading strategies with students by singing the song on page 128.	

***Note:** For more tips, engagement strategies, and fluency options to include in this lesson, see pages 122–128.

Name:____________________ Date:____________

How Plants Grow

Do you know how plants grow? First, there is a seed. It is under the ground. Next, roots grow down into the soil. The roots get food and water for the plant. Then, the stem begins to grow above the ground. The stem grows up, up, up. Leaves grow on the stem. The leaves need the sun to make food for the plant. Some plants get flowers. We can watch plants grow. We can watch them grow tall.

Name: ______________________ Date: ____________

"How Plants Grow" Response

Directions: Reread the text on page 66 to answer each question.

1. Where do roots grow?

   (A) The roots grow above the ground.

   (B) The roots grow down into the soil.

   (C) The roots grow up, up, up.

   (D) The text does not say.

2. What words does the author use instead of the word *dirt*?

3. What happens after the stem begins to grow above the ground?

Fiction Text Teacher Notes

Planting, Waiting, Growing

	Lesson Steps	Teacher Think Alouds
Ready, Set, Predict!	• Provide the text to students and display a larger version. • Read the title of the poem aloud to students and ask them to predict what the poem will be about. Ask students to pair-share any prior knowledge they have about plants and how they grow.	"Before I start to read about a topic, I think of all the things I already know about the topic. This helps me understand what I am about to read."
Go!	• Read the poem aloud once through without stopping. Model fluent reading with expression. Have students follow along as you read the text. • Discuss with students how reading fluently helps convey meaning and interest. Have students work in pairs to practice reading the poem with good fluency.	"Do you notice how I pause between each stanza? How does the pause help you better understand the text?"
Reread to Clarify	• Ask students to reread the text independently to clarify. Tell them to circle any words or sentences they want to clarify. Pair students to discuss the items they circle. • Draw students' attention to the line, *Gather up the food*. Ask partners to think about why the author says this. Invite them to discuss using the following: *After rereading the text, I think the author says,* Gather up the food *because* ______.	
Reread to Question	• Explain that authors make choices about which words they use as they are writing. Ask students to reread the text and highlight words that tell about the author's feelings about growing plants. • Pair students and have them question each other on the words they highlighted: *Why did the author use the word* _____ *to describe* _____? or *How does the word* _____ *help the reader understand* _____? • Have students respond to the question and prompts on page 70.	"Why does the author use the words *fun* and *joy* in the poem? I think she uses these words to tell me how she feels about growing plants."
Reread to Summarize and Respond	• Provide pairs of students with paper. Have them reread the text to summarize by drawing pictures to sequence the events that happen in the poem. • Review the close reading strategies with students by singing the song on page 128.	

***Note:** For more tips, engagement strategies, and fluency options to include in this lesson, see pages 122–128.

Name: ______________________ Date: ______________

Planting, Waiting, Growing

By Katrina E. Housel

Dig a hole in the ground
And put seeds all around.

Let the plants have some sun.
Gardening is fun!

Give water to the shoots
To help them grow their roots.

Gather up the food.
Fruits and veggies to be chewed.

Give your friends the spare.
And spread joy everywhere!

Name: ______________________________ Date: ______________

"Planting, Waiting, Growing" Response

Directions: Reread the poem on page 69 to answer each question.

1. The author suggests spreading joy by doing what?

   Ⓐ planting a garden with a friend

   Ⓑ sharing the extra fruits and vegetables

   Ⓒ eating fruits and vegetables

   Ⓓ taking care of the plants in a garden

2. What does the author tell you about the setting? Give an example.

   ____

   ____

   ____

3. How does the author feel about gardening? How do you know?

   ____

   ____

   ____

Name: ______________________ Date: ______________

Let's Compare!

Plants' Needs

Directions: Think about what plants need. Copy lines from both texts that tell about each need.

	Planting, Waiting, Growing	How Plants Grow
soil/ ground		
water		
sun		

Thinking About Plants!

Teacher Directions: Cut apart the cards. Read each activity to decide whether students should complete one, two, three, or four activities and whether they should complete them independently, in pairs, in small groups, or as a whole class for a shared experience.

Radical Reading

Circle all the location and direction words in "How Plants Grow." Practice changing your voice to make it sound like the location or direction of each word. For example, the word *up* could be read in a high voice.

Fun Fluency

Reread the poem, "Planting, Waiting, Growing" with a partner. Practice reading the poem as your partner acts it out. Then, switch roles.

Wonderful Words

The author uses the words *fun* and *joy* in the poem "Planting, Waiting, Growing." Make a list of five more words that the author could have used to show that she likes plants.

Wacky Writing

The nonfiction text tells about how plants grow. Think about how you have grown since you were a baby. Write sentences to tell about it. Give your writing the title "How Kids Grow."

Unit 8 Overview

Seasons

Theme Summary

Winter, spring, summer, and fall—as adults, we dress, celebrate holidays, and do activities by the season. Young children are beginning to understand the weather and cultural implications of the seasons. This unit gives students an opportunity to look more in depth at what happens to a tree during several seasons and to think about temperature and other changes that each season brings.

Standards

- Identify who is telling the story at various points in a text.
- Identify the main topic and retell key details of a text.
- Know that short-term weather conditions can change daily, and weather patterns change over the seasons.

Materials

- *The Seasons* (page 75)
- *"The Seasons" Response* (page 76)
- *If I Were a Tree* (page 78)
- *"If I Were a Tree" Response* (page 79)
- *Let's Compare! The Seasons of a Tree* (page 80)
- *Thinking About Seasons!* (page 81)
- pencils
- crayons
- paper

Comparing the Texts

After students complete the lessons for each text, have them work in pairs or groups to reread both texts and complete the *Let's Compare! The Seasons of a Tree* activity page (page 80). Finally, students can work to complete the *Thinking About Seasons!* matrix (page 81). The matrix activities allow students to work on the important literacy skills of reading, writing, vocabulary, and fluency. **Note:** Be sure to read each activity prior to implementation to see if it's intended for students to complete independently, in pairs, in small groups, or as a whole class for a shared experience. Make adjustments to the activities according to students' abilities.

Answer Key

"The Seasons" Response (page 76)

1. C. weather
2. Answers will vary. Responses should include that it is windy in spring, and wind is needed for flying a kite.
3. Answers will vary. Students' responses should include that the text says *the leaves change colors and fall off the trees.*

"If I Were a Tree" Response (page 79)

1. B. down deep
2. It means that the tree could grow to be tall and high.
3. The text says *the birds in their nests would all live on me.*

Let's Compare! The Seasons of a Tree (page 80)

Students' trees will vary. For spring, students should include a lot of green leaves. For summer, students should make the tree full of green leaves. For fall, students should include some various colored leaves and not as many leaves. For winter, students should hardly include leaves. They might include snow, too.

Nonfiction Text Teacher Notes

The Seasons

	Lesson Steps	Teacher Think Alouds
 **Ready, Set, Predict!**	• Provide the text to students and display a larger version. Read the title aloud and ask students to use prior knowledge to name the four seasons. • Have students turn to partners and make predictions using the following prompt: *I think I know _____ about the seasons.*	"The title makes me think of the four seasons. The illustrations help confirm that this text will be about the four seasons."
 **Go!**	• Read the text aloud. Model good expression. • Divide students into two groups. Assign one group the warm weather paragraphs and the other group the cool weather paragraphs. Read the text again. Have all students read the opening paragraph. Then, ask them to read the paragraphs they were assigned.	
 **Reread to Clarify**	• Have students reread the text with partners to clarify. Ask them to underline any words or ideas they want to clarify. Have students discuss anything they circle with their partners. • Discuss the layout of the text. Have students reread the text to identify the main topic and detail sentences about the seasons. Have students use a differently colored crayon to identify and underline the sentences that relate to each particular season.	"Knowing the structure of the text helps me know how to read and better understand it. Pausing before starting to read about a new season helps keep the information about each season separate."
Reread to Question	• Divide students into small groups and have them reread the text to question. One student should choose a season and role-play an activity or event from the season. The other students can ask questions as they guess which season the person is role-playing. Allow every student an opportunity to role-play and guess. • Have students respond to the question and prompts on page 76.	
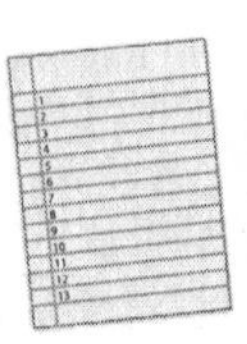 **Reread to Summarize and Respond**	• Provide students with paper. Have them fold the paper into four sections and label each section with the name of a season. • Ask students to reread the text to summarize by writing or drawing one event from the text and one from their prior knowledge for each season.	"The text describes things that happen in each season. It reminds me about other things that happen during each season."

***Note:** For more tips, engagement strategies, and fluency options to include in this lesson, see pages 122–128.

Name: ______________________ Date: ______________

The Seasons

By Kathleen Kopp

What do you think of when you think of spring, summer, autumn, and winter? These are Earth's seasons. The weather is different in each season.

Spring usually means lots of rain. Warmer weather makes the snow and ice melt. New plants sprout. The weather can be windy. It is a good time to fly a kite.

The weather in the **summer** is hot. Plants grow a lot in this season. Children like to swim and play in the water to keep cool.

In **autumn**, the weather gets cooler. The leaves change colors and fall off the trees. Animals get ready for winter.

Winter can be very cold. It brings snow in some places. Many animals sleep during the winter. It is fun for children to play in the snow. They can build snowmen. In other places it does not snow.

Name: ______________________ Date: ______________

"The Seasons" Response

Directions: Reread the text on page 75 to answer each question.

1. The opening sentences tell the reader the text will describe which of the following about each season?

   Ⓐ temperatures
   Ⓑ months
   Ⓒ weather
   Ⓓ activities

2. What evidence is there that spring is a good time to fly a kite?

3. How does the author describe what happens to trees in autumn?

Science Texts

Fiction Text Teacher Notes

If I Were a Tree

	Lesson Steps	Teacher Think Alouds
Ready, Set, Predict!	• Provide the text to students and display a larger version. • Introduce the poem by reading the title and author. Draw students' attention to the three stanzas of the poem. • Have students do a quick and quiet text walk to familiarize themselves with the poem and to identify whether or not the poem has rhyming lines.	"When I read a poem, if it has rhyming words, I emphasize the rhyming words when I come to them. I think this poem will rhyme because I see the words *deep* and *sleep*, and they rhyme."
Go!	• Read the poem aloud to students. Model good expression as you reread lines that lend themselves to expression. • Reread the poem, having students echo-read the poem with you. Discuss how you use expression as you read. • Pair students to practice experimenting with various ways to read the words and lines.	"When the text talks about trees growing high and touching the sky, I make my voice go high also as I read those words."
Reread to Clarify	• Have students reread the poem independently to clarify. Ask them to circle any ideas they do not understand and want to clarify. • Discuss the unusual perspective the poem is written from. Students should underline the pronoun *I* used throughout the poem. • Ask students to emphasize the word *I* as they reread the text with partners.	"The title and first line of the poem make me realize the author is speaking as if she were a tree and not a person. This helps me to better understand the poem."
Reread to Question	• Pair students to reread the poem and ask each other questions about it. Provide the following to support students as they pose questions to each other: Stanza 1: Ask your partner a *what* question. Stanza 2: Ask your partner a *when* question. Stanza 3: Ask your partner a *why* question. • Have students respond to the question and prompts on page 79.	
Reread to Summarize and Respond	• Tell students to reread the text to summarize. Ask students to identify the seasons specifically named in the poem. Challenge students to write two sentences about what they would say about spring and winter if they were trees. • Review the close reading strategies with students by singing the song on page 128.	

Name:________________________ Date:______________

If I Were a Tree

If I were a tree,
I'd grow straight and high.
And touch my branches
way up to the sky.

I would dig my roots
down far and down deep.
I'd grow in the spring.
In winter I'd sleep.

The birds in their nests
would all live on me.
I'd be so happy
if I were a tree.

Name: ______________________ Date: ______________

"If I Were a Tree" Response

Directions: Reread the poem on page 78 to answer each question.

1. Which words in the text describe where roots grow?

   Ⓐ straight and high

   Ⓑ down deep

   Ⓒ up to the sky

   Ⓓ I'd sleep

2. What does the phrase *and touch my branches way up to the sky* mean?

3. Use the text to describe how birds use trees.

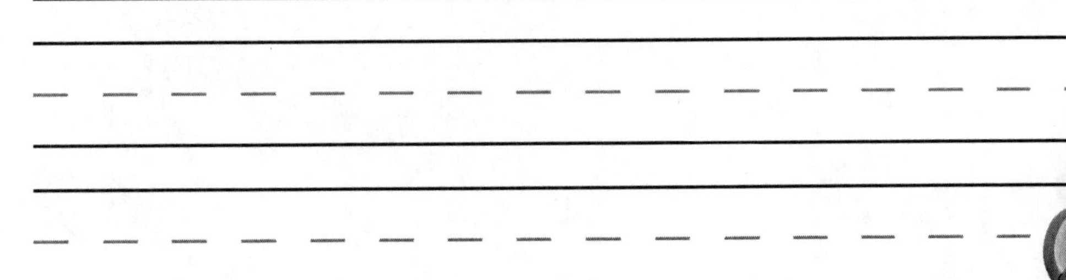

Name: ______________________ Date: ______________

Let's Compare!

The Seasons of a Tree

Directions: Add details to the tree branches to show what the tree looks like in each season. Use information from both texts as well as prior knowledge to help you.

Spring

Summer

Autumn

Winter

Thinking About Seasons

Teacher Directions: Cut apart the cards. Read each activity to decide whether students should complete one, two, three, or four activities and whether they should complete them independently, in pairs, in small groups, or as a whole class for a shared experience.

Radical Reading

Reread the poem. Mark the symbol # next to sentences that tell what happens to the tree during one of the seasons.

Fun Fluency

Choose either the poem or the nonfiction text. Practice reading it several times. Read it aloud to a kindergarten class or a small group of your classmates.

Wonderful Words

Fold a sheet of paper into four sections. Label each section with the name of a season. Write words from the texts that describe each season. Add other words you know to each season.

Wacky Writing

Choose another living thing such as a plant or an animal. Write what would happen to it during each season. Challenge yourself to write from the perspective of the plant or animal.

Unit 9 Overview

The Giant Moon

Theme Summary

Objects in the sky have fascinated and caused wonder since the beginning of humankind. The focus of this unit is the moon. We know that the moon's shape stays the same, but observe it for a month, and it appears to change. This unit pairs a familiar nursery rhyme with a nonfiction text on the moon, though it will take on a whole new meaning as students think about the phases of the moon.

Answer Key

"The Moon" Response (page 85)

1. B. The moon reflects light from the sun.
2. Answers will vary. Responses may include that the *moon will go through phases* or that it appears to change *in size and shape*.
3. Answers will vary. Students should include that the pictures help the reader understand the phases better by showing them in pictures. The pictures support the words.

"Hey Diddle Diddle" Response (page 88)

1. B. an action in the poem
2. Check that responses describe the moon as a crescent shape.
3. Students' responses will vary. Be sure that the responses include silly events from the rhyme and reasons why they are the funniest.

Let's Compare! Jumping Over the Moon (page 89)

1. full
2. half
3. crescent
4. new

Standards

- Use illustrations and details in a story to describe its characters, setting, or events.
- Use the illustrations and details in a text to describe its key ideas.
- Know the basic patterns of the sun and moon.

Materials

- *The Moon* (page 84)
- *"The Moon" Response* (page 85)
- *Hey Diddle Diddle* (page 87)
- *"Hey Diddle Diddle" Response* (page 88)
- *Let's Compare! Jumping Over the Moon* (page 89)
- *Thinking About the Moon!* (page 90)
- pencils

Comparing the Texts

After students complete the lessons for each text, have them work in pairs or groups to reread both texts and complete the *Let's Compare! Jumping Over the Moon* activity page (page 89). Finally, students can work to complete the *Thinking About the Moon!* matrix (page 90). The matrix activities allow students to work on the important literacy skills of reading, writing, vocabulary, and fluency. **Note:** Be sure to read each activity prior to implementation to see if it's intended for students to complete independently, in pairs, in small groups, or as a whole class for a shared experience. Make adjustments to the activities according to students' abilities.

Nonfiction Text Teacher Notes

The Moon

	Lesson Steps	Teacher Think Alouds
Ready, Set, Predict!	• Provide students with the text and display a larger version. Ask them to do a quick and quiet text walk. Have students determine the type of text it is and how it is organized. • Ask them to predict the author's purpose for writing the text using the following: *I think the author wrote this text to* (e.g., *persuade, inform, entertain*) *because* _____.	"I think the author wrote this text to inform because I see real photographs of the moon and read about what the moon looks like at different times of the month."
Go!	• Read the text aloud once through without stopping. Tell students to follow along as you read the text. • Have students underline information on the four phases of the moon as they reread the text independently.	
Reread to Clarify	• Group students to reread the text again to clarify. Ask students to circle any ideas they want to learn. Have them discuss anything they circle with their groups. • Tell partners to respond to the following: *The concept that the moon does not make its own light is tricky, so I* _____.	"I read that the moon reflects the light of the sun. I can use what I already know about the word *reflect* to help me understand and clarify what happens with the moon and the sun."
Reread to Question	• Ask students, "How do the pictures support your understanding of the text?" Challenge students to think of other objects that are the shapes of the moon phases. • Pair students. Have them reread the text to question. Tell them to ask each other questions about the phases of the moon using the following: *In which phase* _____*?* • Have students respond to the question and prompts on page 85.	"The crescent moon reminds me of a croissant, a type of bread or roll, because they are the same shape. Making this connection will help me remember the name of this moon phase."
Reread to Summarize and Respond	• Provide time for students to reread the text to summarize by writing two or three sentences that tell the most important things the author wants readers to know about the moon. • Review the close reading strategies with students by singing the song on page 128.	

***Note:** For more tips, engagement strategies, and fluency options to include in this lesson, see pages 122–128.

Name:________________ Date:____________

The Moon

By Christine Dugan

We can see many objects from Earth at night. The moon is the closest and brightest. But the moon does not make its own light. The moon just reflects the light of the sun. What we see as moonlight is actually reflected sunlight.

Watch the sky for a month. The moon will go through phases. This makes it seem as if the moon changes in size and shape. This is because we can only see part of the moon. We see the sunlit part that faces Earth.

During a full moon, we can see all of the moon's sunlit surface.

During a half moon, we see only half of the moon's sunlit surface.

During a crescent moon, we see only a sliver of the moon's sunlit surface.

On some nights, we see no moon at all! This is called a *new moon*.

Name: ______________________ Date: ______________

"The Moon" Response

Directions: Reread the text on page 84 to answer each question.

1. Which sentence best describes how the moon gets its light?

   Ⓐ The moon is the closest and brightest object in the night sky.

   Ⓑ The moon reflects light from the sun.

   Ⓒ The moon goes through phases where we can see parts of the lit moon.

   Ⓓ The phases of the moon make it seem as if the moon changes size and shape.

2. Use evidence from the text to describe what happens to the moon if it is watched for a whole month.

3. Describe how the pictures contribute to the reader's understanding of the text.

Fiction Text Teacher Notes

Hey Diddle Diddle

	Lesson Steps	Teacher Think Alouds
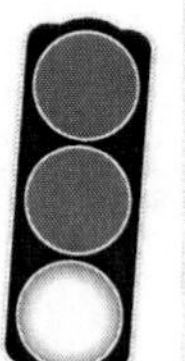 **Ready, Set, Predict!**	• Provide students with the text and display a larger version. Read the title aloud to students. Ask if students are familiar with this traditional nursery rhyme, and discuss any prior knowledge students have with the rhyme. • Tell students that some of the characters are not traditional characters. Ask students to use the illustrations to describe the characters in the rhyme.	"I see a cat playing a fiddle and a cow jumping over the moon. These must be characters in the rhyme."
 **Go!**	• Read the text aloud to students. Encourage students who are familiar with the rhyme to read or recite it with you. • Tell students to independently reread the text. Challenge students to circle the longest word and the shortest word.	
 **Reread to Clarify**	• Have students reread the text in small groups to clarify. Ask them to underline words or sentences they want to clarify. Provide the following sentence frames to help them: *I didn't understand the word _____, so I _____* and *I didn't get the _____, so I _____.*	"I don't understand the word *fiddle*, so I look at the illustration and see the cat playing an instrument. Now I know that a fiddle is like a violin."
 **Reread to Question**	• Divide students into groups of four. Assign each student in the group one of the events from the rhyme. Ask them to reread the text to question by asking each other why each event happened. *Why do you think the cow jumped over the moon?* Other students can speculate as they offer answers. • Have students respond to the question and prompts on page 88.	
Reread to Summarize and Respond	• Group students to reread the text to summarize by writing new versions of the rhyme. Students can make their poems rhyme, but if they cannot, have them focus on the characters and events. Ask students to share their newly created versions with the entire class. • Review the close reading strategies with students by singing the song on page 128.	"Before I begin creating a new version, I first think of the characters and the events I want to include."

***Note:** For more tips, engagement strategies, and fluency options to include in this lesson, see pages 122–128.

Name: ______________________ Date: ______________

Hey Diddle Diddle

Traditional

Hey diddle diddle
The cat and the fiddle,
The cow jumped over the moon.
The little dog laughed to see such sport,
And the dish ran away with the spoon.

Name: ______________________________ Date: ______________

"Hey Diddle Diddle" Response

Directions: Reread the nursery rhyme on page 87 to answer each question.

1. What does the word *sport* mean in the text?

   Ⓐ soccer

   Ⓑ an action in the poem

   Ⓒ a drink

   Ⓓ to wear

2. Describe the shape of the moon shown in the illustration.

3. In your opinion, what is the funniest event in the poem and why?

Name: ______________________ Date: ______________

Let's Compare!

Jumping Over the Moon

Directions: Circle the correct label under each picture of the moon. Use "The Moon" to help you know what each phase looks like.

1\.

crescent full

2\.

new half

3\.

half crescent

4\.

new full

Thinking About the Moon!

Teacher Directions: Cut apart the cards. Read each activity to decide whether students should complete one, two, three, or four activities and whether they should complete them independently, in pairs, in small groups, or as a whole class for a shared experience.

Radical Reading

Create a hand movement to go with each line of the nursery rhyme. Practice reading the rhyme several times while doing the hand movements. Go to a kindergarten classroom and perform the rhyme. Then, teach them the hand movements, too!

Fun Fluency

Reread the descriptions of the phases of the moon in the nonfiction text with a partner. One partner reads the phrase up to the comma. The other partner reads the description of what the phase looks like. Practice together until it can be read smoothly.

Wonderful Words

Reread the nursery rhyme to find:

- the words that are animals
- the verbs
- the word that is an instrument
- the word that is a utensil

Wacky Writing

Create a moon observation journal. Observe the moon at least two nights during the month. Draw a picture of the moon each time you see it. Add sentences to your pictures.

American Symbols

Theme Summary

No statue symbolizes freedom more than the Statue of Liberty. This text pair provides students with two ways of learning more about the statue. Students get to experience the life of an immigrant seeing the statue for the first time in the fictional reader's theater script. The nonfiction text provides background information about the statue. Through both of these texts, students will learn about how the statue symbolizes freedom.

Standards

- Compare and contrast the adventures and experiences of characters in stories.
- Identify the main topic and retell key details of a text.
- Know the history of American symbols.

Materials

- *Meet Lady Liberty* (page 93)
- *"Meet Lady Liberty" Response* (page 94)
- *Coming to America* (page 96)
- *"Coming to America" Response* (page 97)
- *Let's Compare! Use Both Texts* (page 98)
- *Thinking About American Symbols!* (page 99)
- pencils
- green crayons

Comparing the Texts

After students complete the lessons for each text, have them work in pairs or groups to reread both texts and complete the *Let's Compare! Use Both Texts* activity page (page 98). Finally, students can work to complete the *Thinking About American Symbols!* matrix (page 99). The matrix activities allow students to work on the important literacy skills of reading, writing, vocabulary, and fluency. **Note:** Be sure to read each activity prior to implementation to see if it's intended for students to complete independently, in pairs, in small groups, or as a whole class for a shared experience. Make adjustments to the activities according to students' abilities.

Answer Key

"Meet Lady Liberty" Response (page 94)

1. D. She is 305 feet tall.
2. Answers will vary but may include that *liberty means freedom*, so the Statue of Liberty means the statue of freedom.
3. The text says there is *a crown on her head*, and that she *holds a book*.

"Coming to America" Response (page 97)

1. B. She was packed up in many wooden crates.
2. Sophia describes the statue as a princess because there is a crown on the statue's head.
3. The Captain's son said his father saw with his own eyes the ship that the statue was on.

Let's Compare! Use Both Texts (page 98)

Answer	Coming to America	Meet Lady Liberty
1. France		X
2. 214 crates	X	
3. 305 feet		X
4. Lady Liberty	X	X
5. freedom		X

Nonfiction Text Teacher Notes

Meet Lady Liberty

	Lesson Steps	Teacher Think Alouds
Ready, Set, Predict!	• Provide students with the text and display a larger version. Have them do a quick and quiet text walk. • Ask students to make predictions using the following prompt: *I think the author wrote this text to* _____ (e.g., *inform, persuade, entertain*) *because* _____.	"When I read a text, I think about why the author wrote it. I think about whether it is informing me about something, trying to persuade or convince me of something, or if it is entertaining."
Go!	• Read the text aloud to students as they follow along. Model fluent reading. • Allow students time to review their predictions about why the author wrote the text. Allow students to revise their statements and/or reasons, as needed. • Choral-read the text together as a class.	
Reread to Clarify	• Pair students and have them reread the text to clarify. They should underline words that are difficult for them and discuss the words with their partners using the following: *The word* _____ *is tricky, so I* _____ (e.g., *sound it out, look for parts I know, reread, read on*).	
Reread to Question	• Invite students to reread the text with partners to question. Ask them to circle the title and underline phrases or sentences that are details that help clarify the main idea. • Tell students that some of the details tell about the statue being a gift and others tell about how she looks. Have students ask each other questions about the details they underline such as *Does*_____ *tell about the statue as a gift?* and *Does* _____ *tell about how the statue looks?* • Have students respond to the question and prompts on page 94.	"The title of a text often tells the main idea. The title is 'Meet Lady Liberty.' I look to see if the sentences in the text tell details about the Statue of Liberty."
Reread to Summarize and Respond 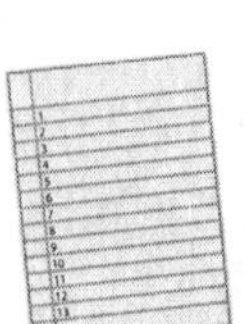	• Tell students to reread the text to summarize. Have students look at the image of the Statue of Liberty on the page and identify on the picture all the parts described in the text. Have students label the illustration. Assist students in finding out more about the statue and label other parts.	"When I read a description of how the Statue of Liberty looks and I see an illustration of the statue, I try to find the parts that are described."

Name: ______________________________ Date: ______________________

Meet Lady Liberty

By Sharon Coan

The Statue of Liberty is a symbol of the United States. France gave the United States a gift. The gift was a statue—the Statue of Liberty. We call her Lady Liberty. Liberty means freedom. Lady Liberty came on a ship in many parts. When they put her together, she was 305 feet (93 meters) tall. A crown is on her head. She holds a book. She is proud. She shows that Americans are free.

Name: ______________________ Date: ______________

"Meet Lady Liberty" Response

Directions: Reread the text on page 93 to answer each question.

1. What detail is given to show how large the Statue of Liberty is?

   Ⓐ A crown is on her head.

   Ⓑ She holds a book.

   Ⓒ We call her Lady Liberty.

   Ⓓ She is 305 feet (93 meters) tall.

2. What evidence is there for why the statue symbolizes freedom?

3. Use the text to describe how the Statue of Liberty looks.

Fiction Text Teacher Notes

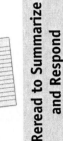

Coming to America

	Lesson Steps	Teacher Think Alouds
 **Ready, Set, Predict!**	• Provide students with the text and display a larger version. Discuss the format of the reader's theater script with students. • Ask students to make predictions using the following: *I think the author wrote this text as a reader's theater script because _____.*	"This text is not in paragraph format. It is written like characters are talking to each other. The names of the characters are on the left. The words they say are on the right. This tells me it must be a play or a drama."
 **Go!**	• Read the entire reader's theater script aloud. Model changing your voice for each character so students become familiar with each of the parts. • Divide the class into six groups. Assign each group one part of the script. Read through the script with students reading their assigned parts.	
 **Reread to Clarify**	• Draw students' attention to the sentence where Sophia states, *I want to be a whole family again—instead of in pieces.* Ask students to reread the text to clarify by underlining phrases or ideas that help clarify Sophia's statement. • Tell students to work with partners to underline words that describe the Statue of Liberty with green crayons.	"If something is tricky in a story, I can look for clues about what it means in other parts of the story. I read that the family is in pieces. Sophia misses her papa. The dad is not a character in the reader's theater script. The dad must not be with the family on the boat, so the family is not all together."
Reread to Question	• Create a list of the characters in the script. Have students reread the text to determine the relationship of each character (i.e., *brother, Captain of the boat*). List this information next to each person's name. • Tell students to work together to ask questions of each other about the characters and their experiences with the Statue of Liberty such as *What is _____'s reaction to the Statue of Liberty?* and *Who has/has not seen the statue before?* • Have students respond to the question and prompts on page 97.	"Francis reacts to seeing the statue with amazement when he uses the word *Wow*! It seems to be his first time seeing the statue."
 **Reread to Summarize and Respond**	• Ask students to pretend to be one of the characters from the script. Have them reread the text to summarize by writing diary entries for the day the reader's theater script takes place. • Review the close reading strategies with students by singing the song on page 128.	

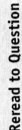

Social Studies Texts

Name: ______________________ Date: ______________

Coming to America

By Kathleen E. Bradley

Narrator: A ferry sails through New York Harbor. The Statue of Liberty can be seen briefly through gaps in the morning fog.

Sophia: Oh, she's beautiful—a princess! Do you see her crown?

Francis: Wow! Yes, I see her now. She is very big! Papa said that when we see the Statue of Liberty, we've made it to America.

Mama: That's true. It won't be long before we see Papa, too.

Sophia: I miss Papa. It's been so long. I want to be a whole family again—instead of in pieces.

Captain: The statue knows how that feels. Lady Liberty also came to America in pieces. She was packed up in many wooden crates.

Captain's Son: Two hundred fourteen crates to be exact. She was brought here on a ship from France. My father saw the crates with his own eyes.

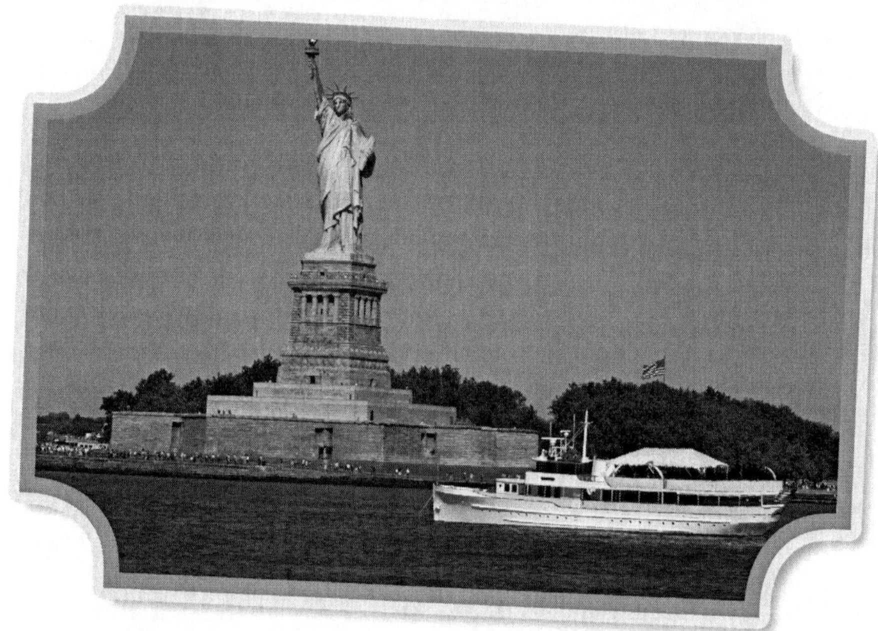

Name: ______________________ Date: ______________

"Coming to America" Response

Directions: Reread the script on page 96 to answer each question.

1. Which sentence supports the idea that the statue came in pieces?

   Ⓐ She was brought on a ship.

   Ⓑ She was packed up in many wooden crates.

   Ⓒ The family wants to be whole again.

   Ⓓ She is very big!

2. Why does Sophia describe the statue as a princess?

3. How does the captain know about the Statue of Liberty?

Name:______________________ Date:______________

Let's Compare!

Use Both Texts

Directions: Use evidence from both texts to answer the questions. Put an *X* in each row to show which text you found the answer in.

Question	Answer	Coming to America	Meet Lady Liberty
1. What country gave the statue to the United States?			
2. How many crates was the statue packed in?			
3. How tall is the statue?			
4. What is another name for the Statue of Liberty?			
5. What does *liberty* mean?			

Thinking About American Symbols!

Teacher Directions: Cut apart the cards. Read each activity to decide whether students should complete one, two, three, or four activities and whether they should complete them independently, in pairs, in small groups, or as a whole class for a shared experience.

Radical Reading

Practice reading the "Coming to America" reader's theater script with a group of friends. Each one can play a different part. Perform the script for another class after you have practiced.

Fun Fluency

Practice reading the "Coming to America" reader's theater script by yourself. Try to use a different voice for each character. After you have practiced, perform your version for a friend.

Wonderful Words

Look at a picture of the Statue of Liberty. What words do you think of when you see her? Make a list.

Wacky Writing

Write about what you would say if it was your first time seeing the Statue of Liberty. You can write it as a paragraph or as a reader's theater script.

Unit 11 Overview

Maps

Theme Summary

X marks the spot! At least that's what the pirates say. Students will have fun learning about maps as they read about children on a treasure hunt using a map at a birthday party. The nonfiction text gives students information about what maps are and the features they include. Students will be anxious to get started learning about maps with this unit!

Answer Key

"Picturing Our World" Response (page 103)

1. A. key
2. Answers will vary. Students may choose the sentence: *A map is a small picture of a large area.* Students should support their answers with reasons.
3. The compass rose shows the direction: north, east, south, west.

"Follow That Map!" Response (page 106)

1. C. at the third place
2. Answers will vary. Students may include that there is a Start sign at the beginning of the path and that the first dashed line ends up at the symbol for the painting.
3. The children have to look in a second place because the treasure is not in the first place they look.

Let's Compare! Make a Map (page 107)

Students' maps will vary. Check that students include words and symbols that relate to the pictures of the places they draw.

Standards

- Explain major differences between books that tell stories and books that give information, drawing on a wide reading of a range of text types.
- Ask and answer questions to help determine or clarify the meaning of words and phrases in a text.
- Understand the characteristics and use of maps, globes, and other geographic tools and technologies.

Materials

- *Picturing Our World* (page 102)
- *"Picturing Our World" Response* (page 103)
- *Follow That Map!* (page 105)
- *"Follow That Map!" Response* (page 106)
- *Let's Compare! Make a Map* (page 107)
- *Thinking About Maps!* (page 108)
- pencils
- yellow and brown crayons

Comparing the Texts

After students complete the lessons for each text, have them work in pairs or groups to reread both texts and complete the *Let's Compare! Make a Map* activity page (page 107). Finally, students can work to complete the *Thinking About Maps!* matrix (page 108). The matrix activities allow students to work on the important literacy skills of reading, writing, vocabulary, and fluency. **Note:** Be sure to read each activity prior to implementation to see if it's intended for students to complete independently, in pairs, in small groups, or as a whole class for a shared experience. Make adjustments to the activities according to students' abilities.

Nonfiction Text Teacher Notes

Picturing Our World

	Lesson Steps	Teacher Think Alouds
Ready, Set, Predict!	• Provide students with the text and display a larger version. • Encourage students to do a quick and quiet text walk. Ask them to predict which words they will have difficulty reading because they do not recognize them right away.	"When I skim the text, I see a couple of words that I do not know the meaning of. I am going to pay close attention to those words as I read to try to figure out their meanings."
Go!	• Read the text aloud to students. Model fluent reading. • Lead a discussion on reading fluently and strategies that can be used to figure out words (e.g., *self correction, sounding out*). • Have students practice reading the text with partners.	"Watch how I self-correct the word *legend*. I notice that it doesn't sound right when I pronounce the *g* as /g/, so I reread and try pronouncing it as /j/."
Reread to Clarify	• Tell students to reread the text with partners or in small groups to clarify. Ask them to use yellow crayons to underline words or phrases they want to clarify or words they think would be challenging for a kindergartner. • Provide time for students to discuss the words and phrases they underline. Encourage students to use strategies to clarify them. • Allow several students to share out their underlined parts using the following: *The word/phrase* ______ *is confusing, so I* _____ (e.g., *reread, read on, look at the illustration, ask a friend*).	"The phrase *compass rose* is confusing, so I reread the sentence, *A compass rose shows four directions: north, east, south, and west*. I also look at the map, and I find the picture of something that shows those directions. This helps me know what a compass rose is."
Reread to Question	• Ask students to reread the text to question. Pair students and have them ask one another questions about the text using the following: *Why is* ______ *helpful on a map*? Students should answer the questions they receive. • Have students respond to the question and prompts on page 103.	
Reread to Summarize and Respond	• Tell students to reread the text to summarize. Have them work with partners to circle the parts maps have with brown crayons. Discuss students' circled parts as a class.	

***Note:** For more tips, engagement strategies, and fluency options to include in this lesson, see pages 122–128.

Name: ______________________________ **Date:** ________________

Picturing Our World

By Sandy Phan

Maps help us know where we are. They show Earth's land, water, and places. A map is a small picture of a large area.

Maps have many features. A compass rose shows four directions: north, east, south, and west. Maps also have legends, sometimes called keys. A legend tells you what the symbols, lines, and colors on a map mean. Knowing these features can help you read and better understand maps.

Name: ______________________ Date: ______________

"Picturing Our World" Response

Directions: Reread the text on page 102 to answer each question.

1. What is another name for a legend?

   Ⓐ key
   Ⓑ symbol
   Ⓒ compass rose
   Ⓓ color

2. Which sentence from the text best describes what a map is? Why?

3. What is the purpose of a compass rose?

Fiction Text Teacher Notes

Follow That Map!

	Lesson Steps	Teacher Think Alouds
Ready, Set, Predict! 	• Provide students with the text and display a larger version. • Tell students that good readers make predictions about what the text will be about. • Ask students to predict what this text will be about and if their predictions are based on the text, illustrations, or both. Provide students with the following frame: *I think we will learn about _____ because _____.*	"Before I begin reading, I look over the text and illustrations to see what I already know about the subject and what I can learn from the way the page is organized and the illustrations."
Go! 	• Read the text aloud to students. Model fluent reading, including phrasing. • Have students independently read the text with pencils to look for words they don't know. Use the following prompts to help your students find words: *Find the longest word. Find the word that is the most interesting.* • Pair students and have one student in each pair read the text while the other student follows the map. Then, have students switch roles.	
Reread to Clarify	• Instruct students to reread the text with partners to clarify. Have them look for and circle other words they need clarification on. Provide students with the following: *The word _____ is confusing, so I _____.* Encourage them to help each other use strategies to clarify the words they circled.	"The word *key* is confusing to me because I keep visualizing the key to a door. So, I look at the illustrations and they help clarify that the text is talking about a part of a map and not a key to a door."
Reread to Question 	• Tell students to reread the text to question. Discuss with students that the characters in the story follow a map to three different locations. Ask, "Where did they run to first? Where did they run to next? Where did they run to last?" After each question, have students underline where the answers are found in the text with yellow crayons. • Have students respond to the question and prompts on page 106.	"There is a map in this text, but I do not learn about maps or how to use maps by reading this text. I read about kids having fun at a party."
Reread to Summarize and Respond	• As a class, reread the text to summarize by writing about where the children looked for the treasure. Use the key on the map to tell where the children looked. Follow the lines on the map to name the places in the correct order.	

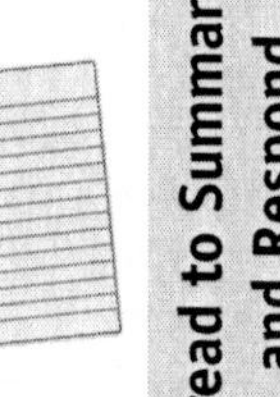

Name: ______________________________ Date: ______________

Follow That Map!

By Sharon Coan

We are at a party. We play games. We have a treasure hunt. We use a map. We follow the map. We use the key.

We run to the first place. We see a painting. The treasure is not here. We run to the second place. We are at the playground. The treasure is not here. We run to the third place. We look for the treasure. The treasure is here!

We used the map. We found the treasure.

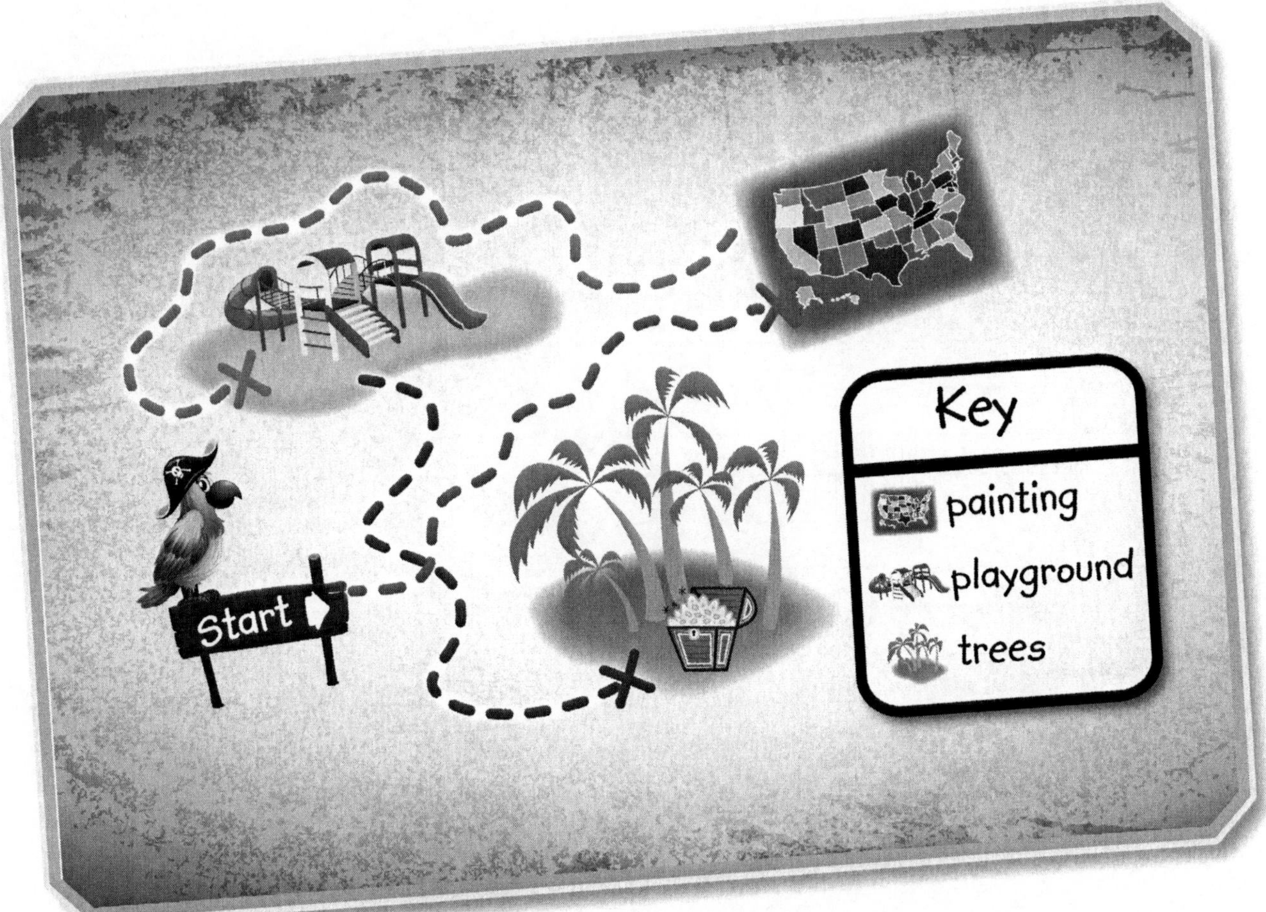

Name: ______________________ Date: ______________

"Follow That Map!" Response

Directions: Reread the text on page 105 to answer each question.

1. Where is the treasure found?

   Ⓐ at the first place
   Ⓑ at the second place
   Ⓒ at the third place
   Ⓓ none of them

2. What evidence is there that the painting is the first place they look?

3. Why do the children have to look in a second place?

Name: ______________________ Date: ______________

Let's Compare!

Make a Map

Directions: Make a treasure map. Draw three places. Then, begin at "Start" and draw a line that connects all of the places. Then, fill in the Key with the names of the places.

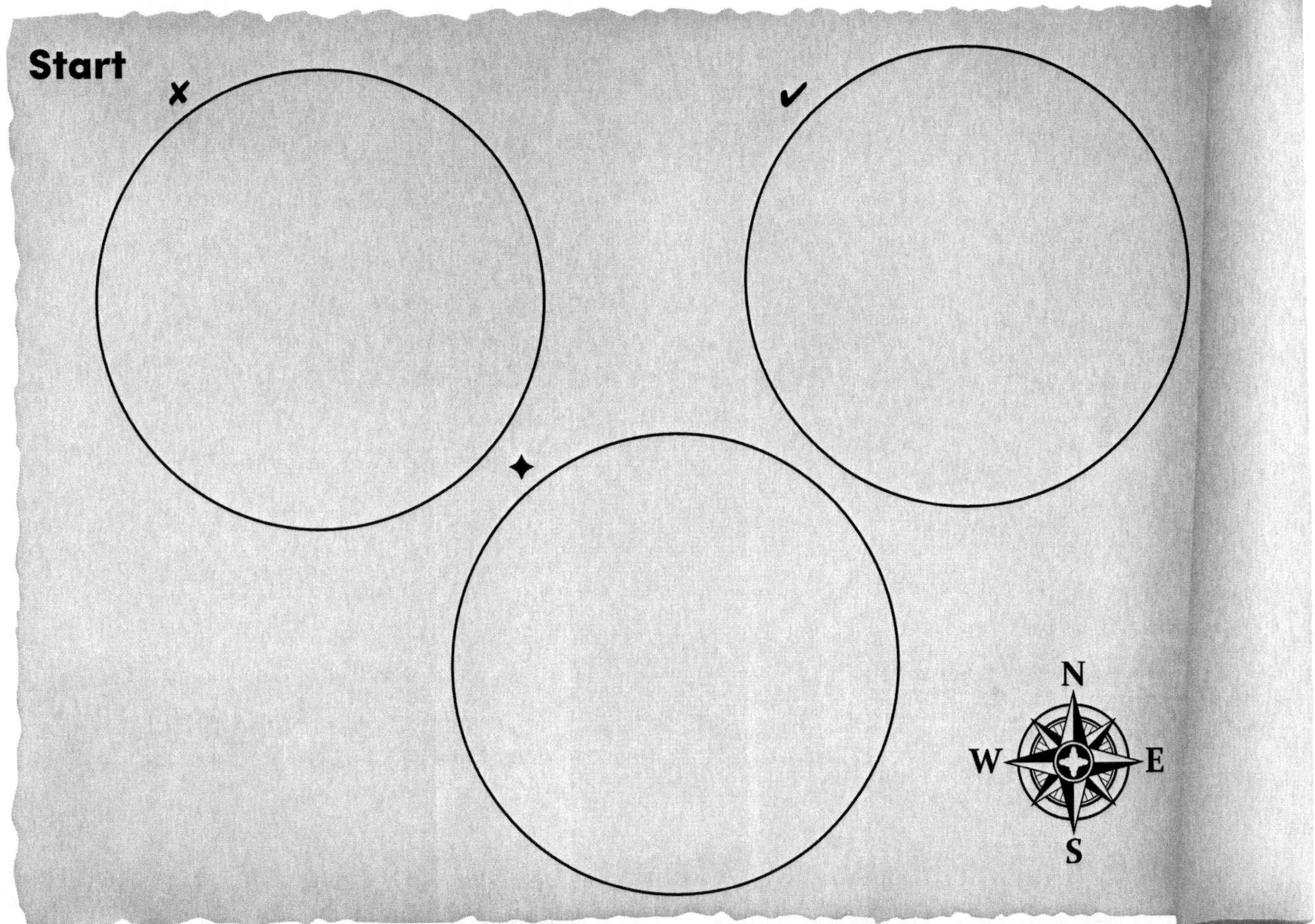

Key

✗ ______________________

✦ ______________________

✔ ______________________

Thinking About Maps!

Teacher Directions: Cut apart the cards. Read each activity to decide whether students should complete one, two, three, or four activities and whether they should complete them independently, in pairs, in small groups, or as a whole class for a shared experience.

Radical Reading

Reread "Follow That Map!" as if you are at the party having fun!

Fun Fluency

Practice reading "Follow That Map!" in your best pirate voice. Perform it for a friend after you have practiced.

Wonderful Words

Maps show many places. What are some places you would like to visit? Make a list of seven places you would love to visit.

Wacky Writing

Pirates like to find gold in treasure boxes. Write about what kind of treasure you would like to find inside the treasure box.

School

Theme Summary

Your students know a lot about being in school. They have been in school now for a couple of years, but do they know how school has changed from times long ago? This pair of texts gets students thinking about being in school—both now and long ago. Some things change a lot and some things never change.

Standards

- Identify words and phrases in stories or poems that suggest feelings or appeal to the senses.
- Describe the connection between two individuals, events, or pieces of information.
- Understand family life today and how it compares with family life in the recent past and family life long ago.

Materials

- *School: Then and Now* (page 111)
- *"School: Then and Now" Response* (page 112)
- *School Days* (page 114)
- *"School Days" Response* (page 115)
- *Let's Compare! My School* (page 116)
- *Thinking About School!* (page 117)
- pencils
- crayons
- drawing paper

Comparing the Texts

After students complete the lessons for each text, have them work in pairs or groups to reread both texts and complete the *Let's Compare! My School* activity page (page 116). Finally, students can work to complete the *Thinking About School!* matrix (page 117). The matrix activities allow students to work on the important literacy skills of reading, writing, vocabulary, and fluency. **Note:** Be sure to read each activity prior to implementation to see if it's intended for students to complete independently, in pairs, in small groups, or as a whole class for a shared experience. Make adjustments to the activities according to students' abilities.

Answer Key

"School: Then and Now" Response (page 112)

1. B. Only rich boys went to school.
2. Answers will vary. Students may include that *Horace Mann changed schools so all children could go*, including rich and poor, and boys and girls. He also made the school year longer.
3. The school year is almost 10 months long *because there is so much more to learn.*

"School Days" Response (page 115)

1. C. summer and autumn
2. Answers will vary. Answers may include any of the following: *chilly winds, crisp fall colors falling down*, or *summer's ending*.
3. The children are described as *yawning in their beds* and *sleepyheads*.

Let's Compare! My School (page 116)

Answers will vary. Check that students' descriptions are related to school.

Nonfiction Text Teacher Notes

School: Then and Now

	Lesson Steps	Teacher Think Alouds
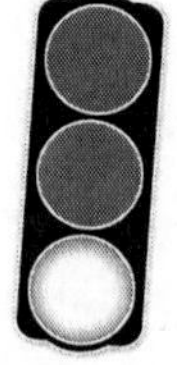 **Ready, Set, Predict!**	• Provide students with the text and display a larger version. • Have students independently skim over the title and text. Ask students to use clues to make predictions on how the text is organized.	"As I skim a text, I think about strategies that can help me understand what I am reading."
 **Go!**	• Read the text aloud to students. Model fluent reading. • Briefly discuss the structure of the text, and then have students reread the text independently. As a class, give a subtitle to summarize the information in each paragraph. Discuss the titles given.	
 **Reread to Clarify**	• Divide students into small groups to reread the text to clarify. Have them circle words or sentences they want to clarify using the prompt, *The word* _____ *is tricky, so I* _____ (e.g., *reread, read on*).	"The word *mattered* is tricky, so I look and see the word *mat* and the *-ed* ending. I pronounce all three parts of the word (*mat, er, ed*) together. Now the word makes sense to me."
 **Reread to Question**	• Invite students to use one crayon color to underline information in the text about who could and couldn't go to school, another color to underline information about the length of the school year, and a third color to underline the subjects studied. • Ask students to reread the text to question. Tell them to create their own questions about how schools have changed using what they underlined. • Have students respond to the question and prompts on page 112.	"I notice that the text names the subjects the boys learned in school long ago, but it does not name the subjects children learn in school today. I can use my knowledge about school to name the subjects we study."
Reread to Summarize and Respond	• Distribute sheets of white paper that has been folded in half to students. • Have students reread the text to summarize by using evidence from the text to draw pictures of what it was like to go to school long ago on one side of the fold and how schools changed because of Horace Mann on the other side of the fold. • Review the close reading strategies with students by singing the song on page 128.	

***Note:** For more tips, engagement strategies, and fluency options to include in this lesson, see pages 122–128.

Name: ________________________ Date: ____________

School: Then and Now

By Karen Donovan

You go to school so you will be ready for life. Long ago, only rich boys went to school. Girls did not go to school at all. The boys went to school for three months each year. They only learned reading, writing, and math.

A man named Horace Mann changed schools so that all children could go. He did not think it mattered if you were a boy or a girl. He thought all students, rich or poor, should learn. He also made the school year longer. Today, the school year is almost 10 months long. That is because there is so much more to learn.

Name: ______________________ Date: ______________

"School: Then and Now" Response

Directions: Reread the text on page 111 to answer each question.

1. What does the author tell about who went to school long ago?

   Ⓐ Only boys went to school.

   Ⓑ Only rich boys went to school.

   Ⓒ Boys and girls went to school.

   Ⓓ Boys did not go to school.

2. Use the text to describe one way Horace Mann changed schools.

3. What reason is given to explain why the school year is almost 10 months long today?

Fiction Text Teacher Notes

School Days

	Lesson Steps	Teacher Think Alouds
Ready, Set, Predict!	• Provide students with the text and display a larger version. Read the title aloud to students and ask students to predict what time of year it will be in the poem based on the title and illustration. Explain that the poem will be about starting a new school year. • Have students share with partners how they feel about going back to school using the sentence frame: *When a new school year begins, I feel* ______.	"When I read the title of a poem, I try to make a connection to the topic by thinking about what I know and how I feel about it. When a new school year begins, I feel excited to see my friends again."
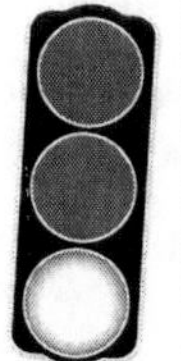 **Go!**	• Read the poem aloud to students. Ask them whether or not the poem has a rhyming structure. • Pair students to reread the poem together. Have students box the rhyming words in the poem. • Discuss with students how knowing where the rhyming words are in the poem affects how the poem is read.	"I see that the rhyming words are at the end of pairs of lines of text. I pause briefly after reading the second line of each pair when reading the poem aloud. This helps the listener understand that the two lines go together."
 **Reread to Clarify**	• Reread the poem aloud to students without the adjectives. Have students circle the adjectives that you skip. Tell students to clarify the circled words. • List the adjectives on the board and have students point to the nouns that the adjectives describe. Help students draw lines from the adjectives to the nouns they describe. • Ask students to discuss with each other how the adjectives clarify the nouns: *How does the adjective* ______ *help you better understand* ______*?*	
 **Reread to Question**	• Tell pairs of students to reread the text to question. Have them ask each other questions about the adjectives they circled and how they appeal to the senses: *Which sense do you think of when you read the word* ______*? How does* ______ *help you visualize* ______*?* • Have students respond to the question and prompts on page 115.	"How do the words *crisp fall colors falling down* help you visualize the season? I can picture red, yellow, and orange leaves all over the ground and falling from the trees."
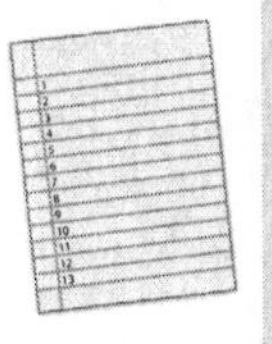  **Reread to Summarize and Respond**	• Divide students into small groups and have them reread the text to summarize. Have one student in each group choose a line from the poem and act it out. The other students in the group should try to guess which line it is. Have students take turns acting out lines.	

Name: ______________________ Date: ______________

School Days

Paper scraps and ink smells,
Summer's ending, tolling bells,
Uniforms and shoe straps,
New blue jeans and baseball caps,

September donning autumn clothes,
Chilly winds and frosted nose,
Crisp fall colors falling down,
School bus rolling into town.
Children yawning in their beds,
It's time for school, sleepyheads!

Name: ______________________________ **Date:** ____________________

"School Days" Response

Directions: Reread the poem on page 114 to answer each question.

1. Which two seasons are in the poem?

   Ⓐ winter and spring
   Ⓑ spring and autumn
   Ⓒ summer and autumn
   Ⓓ winter and summer

2. What evidence is there that the season is autumn?

3. How are children described in the poem?

Name: ______________________ Date: ______________

Let's Compare!

My School

Directions: Reread both texts. Then, complete the web with four sentences that describe the school you go to.

My School

Thinking About School!

Teacher Directions: Cut apart the cards. Read each activity to decide whether students should complete one, two, three, or four activities and whether they should complete them independently, in pairs, in small groups, or as a whole class for a shared experience.

Radical Reading

Reread the poem "School Days." Make a list of things students learn in school besides reading and math.

Fun Fluency

Read the poem "School Days" in a voice that shows excitement to go back to school. Then, read it in a voice that shows sadness that summer is over. Tell a partner which version you liked better and why.

Wonderful Words

Make a list of the things that remind you of school. Share your list with a partner.

Wacky Writing

Horace Mann changed schools in many ways. Write about how you would change school if you could.

References Cited

Brassel, Danny, and Timothy Rasinski. 2008. *Comprehension that Works: Taking Students Beyond Ordinary Understanding to Deep Comprehension*. Huntington Beach, CA: Shell Education.

Common Core State Standards Initiative. 2010. *Common Core State Standards for English Language Arts & Literacy in History/Social Studies, Science, and Technical Subjects*. Washington, DC: National Governors Association Center for Best Practices and the Council of Chief State School Officers.

Fisher, David, and Nancy Frey. 2012. "Close Reading in Elementary Schools." *The Reading Teacher* 66 (3): 179–188.

Hattie, John A. 2008. *Visible Learning: A Synthesis of Over 800 Meta-Analyses Relating to Achievement*. Oxford, UK: Routledge.

Oczkus, Lori D. 2010. *Reciprocal Teaching at Work: Powerful Strategies and Lessons for Improving Reading Comprehension 2nd Edition*. Newark, DE: International Reading Association.

Oczkus, Lori D. 2012. *Just the Facts: Close Reading and Comprehension of Informational Text*. Huntington Beach, CA: Shell Education and International Reading Association (copublication).

Palincsar, Annemarie Sullivan, and Ann L. Brown. 1986. "Interactive Teaching to Promote Independent Learning from Text." *The Reading Teacher* 39 (8): 771–777.

Rasinski, Timothy V. 2010. *The Fluent Reader: Oral and Silent Reading Strategies for Building Fluency, Word Recognition and Comprehension 2nd Edition*. New York: Scholastic.

Rasinski, Timothy V. and Lorraine Griffith. 2010. *Building Fluency Through Practice and Performance*. Huntington Beach, CA: Shell Education.

Rosenshine, Barak, and Carla Meister. 1994. "Reciprocal Teaching: A Review of the Research." *Review of Educational Research* 64 (4): 479–530.

Correlation to the Standards

Shell Education is committed to producing educational materials that are research and standards based. In this effort, we have correlated all of our products to the academic standards of all 50 states, the District of Columbia, the Department of Defense Dependents Schools, and all Canadian provinces.

How to Find Standards Correlations

To print a customized correlation report of this product for your state, visit our website at http://www.shelleducation.com and follow the on-screen directions. If you require assistance in printing correlation reports, please contact our Customer Service Department at 1-877-777-3450.

Purpose and Intent of Standards

Legislation mandates that all states adopt academic standards that identify the skills students will learn in kindergarten through grade twelve. Many states also have standards for Pre–K. This same legislation sets requirements to ensure the standards are detailed and comprehensive.

Standards are designed to focus instruction and guide adoption of curricula. Standards are statements that describe the criteria necessary for students to meet specific academic goals. They define the knowledge, skills, and content students should acquire at each level. Standards are also used to develop standardized tests to evaluate students' academic progress. Teachers are required to demonstrate how their lessons meet state standards. State standards are used in the development of all of our products, so educators can be assured they meet the academic requirements of each state.

Common Core State Standards

The activities in this book are aligned to the Common Core State Standards (CCSS). The chart on page 120 lists the standards addressed in each lesson. Specific standards are also listed on the first page of each lesson.

McREL Compendium

We use the Mid-Continent Research for Education and Learning (McREL) Compendium to create standards correlations. Each year, McREL analyzes state standards and revises the compendium. By following this procedure, McREL is able to produce a general compilation of national standards. Each lesson in this product is based on one or more McREL standards. The chart on page 121 lists the standards addressed in each lesson.

TESOL and WIDA Standards

The activities in this book promote English language development for English language learners. The chart on page 121 lists the standards addressed in each lesson.

Correlation to the Standards *(cont.)*

College and Career Readiness Standards	Lessons
Literacy.RL.1.1—Ask and answer questions about key details in a text.	Plants (p. 64)
Literacy.RL.1.2—Retell stories, including key details, and demonstrate understanding of their central message or lesson.	Time (p. 37)
Literacy.RL.1.3—Describe characters, settings, and major events in a story, using key details.	Turtles (p. 28); Fractions (p. 55)
Literacy.RL.1.4—Identify words and phrases in stories or poems that suggest feelings or appeal to the senses.	Plants (p. 64); School (p. 109)
Literacy.RL.1.5—Explain major differences between books that tell stories and books that give information, drawing on a wide reading of a range of text types.	Maps (p. 100)
Literacy.RL.1.6—Identify who is telling the story at various points in a text.	Baseball (p. 19); Seasons (p. 73)
Literacy.RL.1.7—Use illustrations and details in a story to describe its characters, setting, or events.	Bakeries (p. 10); The Giant Moon (p. 82)
Literacy.RL.1.9—Compare and contrast the adventures and experiences of characters in stories.	American Symbols (p. 91)
Literacy.RL.1.10—With prompting and support, read prose and poetry of appropriate complexity for grade 1.	Collecting and Organizing Data (p. 46)
Literacy.RI.1.2—Identify the main topic and retell key details of a text.	Turtles (p. 28); Seasons (p. 73); American Symbols (p. 91)
Literacy.RI.1.3—Describe the connection between two individuals, events, or pieces of information.	Bakeries (p. 10); School (p. 109)
Literacy.RI.1.4—Ask and answer questions to help determine or clarify the meaning of words and phrases in a text.	Maps (p. 100)
Literacy.RI.1.5—Know and use various text features to locate key facts or information in a text.	Time (p. 37)
Literacy.RI.1.6—Distinguish between information provided by pictures or other illustrations and information provided by the words in a text.	Baseball (p. 19); Collecting and Organizing Data (p. 46)
Literacy.RI.1.7—Use the illustrations and details in a text to describe its key ideas.	Fractions (p. 55); The Giant Moon (p. 82)
Literacy.RF.1.1.d—Use personal, possessive, and indefinite pronouns.	Baseball (p. 19)
Literacy.RF.1.3.f—Read words with inflectional endings.	Turtles (p. 28)
Literacy.RF.1.4—Read with sufficient accuracy and fluency to support comprehension.	Bakeries (p. 10)
Math.Content.1.MD.B.3—Tell and write time in hours and half-hours using analog and digital clocks.	Time (p. 37)

Correlation to the Standards *(cont)*

McREL Standards	Lessons
Science 1.1—Knows that short-term weather conditions can change daily, and weather patterns change over the seasons.	Seasons (p. 73)
Science 3.1—Knows the basic patterns of the Sun and Moon.	The Giant Moon (p. 82)
Science 5.1—Knows the basic needs of plants and animals.	Plants (p. 64)
Geography 1.0—Understands the characteristics and uses of maps, globes, and other geographic tools and technologies.	Maps (p. 100)
History 1.2—Understands family life today and how it compares with family life in the recent past and family life long ago.	School (p. 109)
History 4.8—Knows the history of American symbols.	American Symbols (p. 91)
Math 2.5—Understands the concept of a unit and its subdivision into equal parts.	Fractions (p. 55)
Math 6.1—Collects and represents information about objects or events in simple graphs.	Collecting and Organizing Data (p. 46)

TESOL/WIDA Standards	Lessons
English language learners **communicate** for **social, intercultural,** and **instructional** purposes within the school setting	All Lessons
English language learners **communicate** information, ideas, and concepts necessary for academic success in the area of **language arts**	All Lessons
English language learners **communicate** information, ideas, and concepts necessary for academic success in the area of **mathematics**	All Mathematics Lessons
English language learners **communicate** information, ideas, and concepts necessary for academic success in the area of **science**	All Science Lessons
English language learners **communicate** information, ideas, and concepts necessary for academic success in the area of **social studies**	All Social Studies Lessons

Tips for Implementing the Lessons

Lesson Tips

Below are additional tips and suggestions you may wish to do with students as you implement the lessons.

- Choose 4 to 6 words from each text pair and place them on a word wall for students to observe. Students can complete various word activities with the words.
- Use online resources, such as video clips or audio clips, to help students better understand the content.
- Have students research the authors of some of the texts or research more about the content in the texts so students can gain more knowledge.
- Keep a running list of strategies students use to clarify words, phrases, and ideas. Have the list visible for students to use as they clarify texts (e.g., reread, read on, sound out).
- Choose a long word from a text and present the letters of the word to students in alphabetical order, dividing the letters into consonants and vowels. Guide students to make a series of 5 to 10 words with the letters by giving them word meanings or clues to guess the words.
- Play WORDO with students by having them draw 4 x 4 matrixes. Display 16 to 20 words from the texts. Have students write one word in each box. Randomly select a word and call out its definition. Have each student mark the box the word is in. The first student to get four words in a straight or diagonal line calls out, "Wordo!"
- Invite students to act out words, sentences, or main ideas of a text with or without using their voices. Have the rest of the class guess what is being acted out.

Pacing Tips

Below are suggested options for implementing the lessons with students.

An Ideal Pacing Plan	If Working with Longer Texts
Day 1: Nonfiction text close reading lesson/follow-up activities **Day 2:** Fiction text close reading lesson/follow-up activities **Day 3:** Compare the texts/follow-up activities **Day 4:** Reread texts/follow-up activities **Day 5:** Reread texts/share follow-up activities	**Day 1:** Complete the close reading steps, including predicting, clarifying, questioning, and summarizing, for the first portion of the text. **Day 2:** Run through all four steps again for the second portion of the text. **Note:** The follow-up activities should be done at the conclusion of the entire reading of a text.

Strategies

Engagement Strategies

Make learning memorable by using the following engagement strategies.

Discussion in Pairs

Throughout the lessons, have students talk with partners or groups to enhance comprehension. Conduct whole-group sharing after partners discuss their responses.

Mark or Code with Text Symbols

Have students work independently or in groups to mark the text using symbols to show their thinking. Provide copies of the text for students and display a copy of the text for the class to view as you demonstrate. Symbols may include:

+ main idea √ details # cool idea ☺ favorite part

Have students use different colored pencils, highlighters, or markers as they read. They can circle, underline, or box portions of the text.

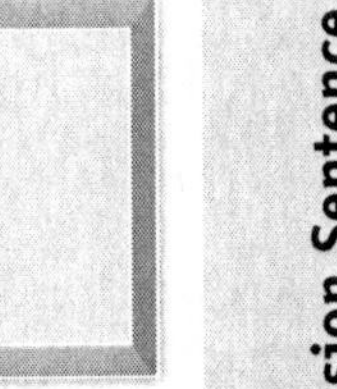

Discussion Sentence Frames

Have students use discussion sentence frames when sharing responses with others. Frames help keep students on task during discussions. Some examples include:

Predict	**Clarify**
I think I will learn ____ because____. *I think the author wrote this because ____.*	*I didn't get the word/sentence ____, so I ____.*
Question	**Summarize**
Who, what, when, where, why, how, I wonder ____.	*This is about ____.* *The main idea is ____.*

Close Reading Props

Bring in a pair of goofy glasses or a magnifying glass to hold up when it is time to read a text closely. You may wish to duplicate the glasses or magnifying glass patterns found on page 126 for students to use during the lessons.

Glasses	**Magnifying Glass**
Tell students, "Close reading is like putting on special glasses as you reread the text to figure it out."	Tell students, "Close reading is like using a magnifying glass to help you understand the text as you reread it."

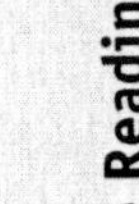

Sing to the Strategies

Help students remember the different purposes for rereading by creating a song with verses for each of the reciprocal teaching strategies. A song option can be found on page 128.

Strategies *(cont.)*

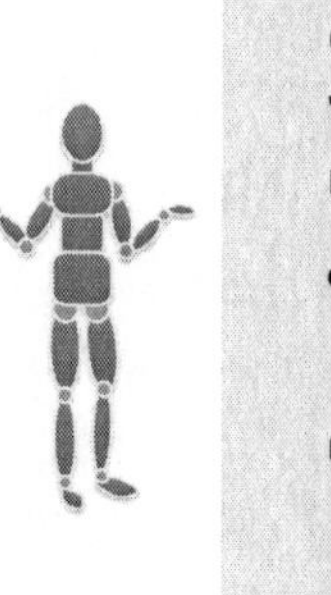

Gestures or Props for Each Strategy		
	Use gestures or props to help students remember the close reading strategies as they closely read a text.	
	Predict: Use a physical crystal ball or pretend to rub a crystal ball to predict what will happen or what the text is about using clues from the text.	**Question:** Use a physical microphone or use a fist to make a microphone to interview one another asking and answering questions.
	Clarify: Use glasses or a magnifying glass. You can also use your arms: parallel to show a "pause" button, point to the left for rewind, and to the right for reading on to help clarify tricky words in a text.	**Summarize:** Use a lasso (with yarn or string) or pretend to wield a lasso to rope in the "main ideas and details" of a text.

Adapted from Lori Oczkus (2010)

Fluency Strategies

The chart below lists various fluency techniques to use with students.

Model Fluent Reading	Teacher or other proficient reader reads the text to students. After the reading, teacher leads students in a discussion of the content of the text *and* the way in which the teacher or reader reads the text (e.g., expression, phrasing, pacing).
Assisted Reading—Choral Reading	Groups of students read the text orally together. Students who are more fluent readers provide an assist to students who are less fluent.
Assisted Reading—Paired Reading	Two readers read a text orally together. One reader is more proficient than the other. The more proficient reader acts as a model for the less fluent one.
Assisted Reading—Audio-recorded Reading	A student reads a text while at the same time listening to a fluent recording of the same text. The recorded reading acts as a model for the student.
Assisted Reading—Echo Reading	Teacher reads the text aloud while tracking the print for students to see. After the text has been read aloud, children imitate, or echo, the teacher as they visually track the text.
Repeated Reading	Students read a text several times orally and silently for different purposes. One purpose for all rereading is to improve students' fluency (e.g., word recognition, automaticity, and expression).
Phrased Text Reading	The teacher or student marks the appropriate phrase boundaries in a text with slash marks. The student then reads the text, pausing at the marked locations. Readers who lack fluency often read in a word-by-word manner that limits the meaning of the passage. These visual cues give students support in reading in meaningful phrases.

Adapted from Timothy Rasinski (2010)

Assessment Options

Aside from students' work on the activity pages, there are many opportunities to assess students during each step of the close reading process. Use the chart below to guide your assessments.

Ready, Set, Predict!

Does the student . . .

- skim the text/visuals to make logical predictions?
- relate relevant prior knowledge?
- anticipate author's purpose?
- predict topic/theme?
- anticipate how the text is organized?

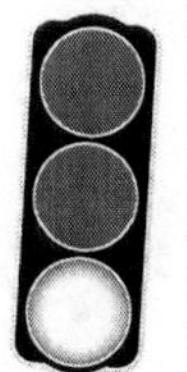

Go!

Does the student . . .

- make an attempt to read the text independently?
- follow along during the teacher read-aloud?
- mark unfamiliar words and ideas?
- participate in shared readings; follow along?
- identify what makes the teacher's reading fluent?

Reread to Clarify

Does the student . . .

- reread to mark words they want to know or clarify?
- identify words/lines that help students visualize?
- identify more than one "fix it" strategy such as sounding out, chopping words into parts, rereading, reading on?

Reread to Question

Does the student . . .

- reread to ask or create questions for peers?
- reread to answer text-dependent questions using text evidence?
- confidently ask and answer questions?

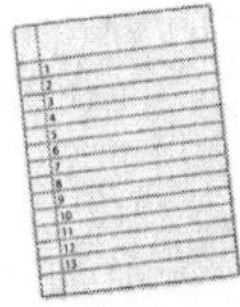

Reread to Summarize and Respond

Does the student . . .

- select main ideas and details to summarize?
- summarize selection in order?
- use key vocabulary to summarize?
- mark text to show responses using symbols?

+ main idea √ details # cool idea ☺ favorite part

- compare/contrast the fiction and nonfiction texts?

Templates

Glasses

Directions: Decorate the glasses. Then, cut them out and glue them on a craft stick. Use them as you closely read text.

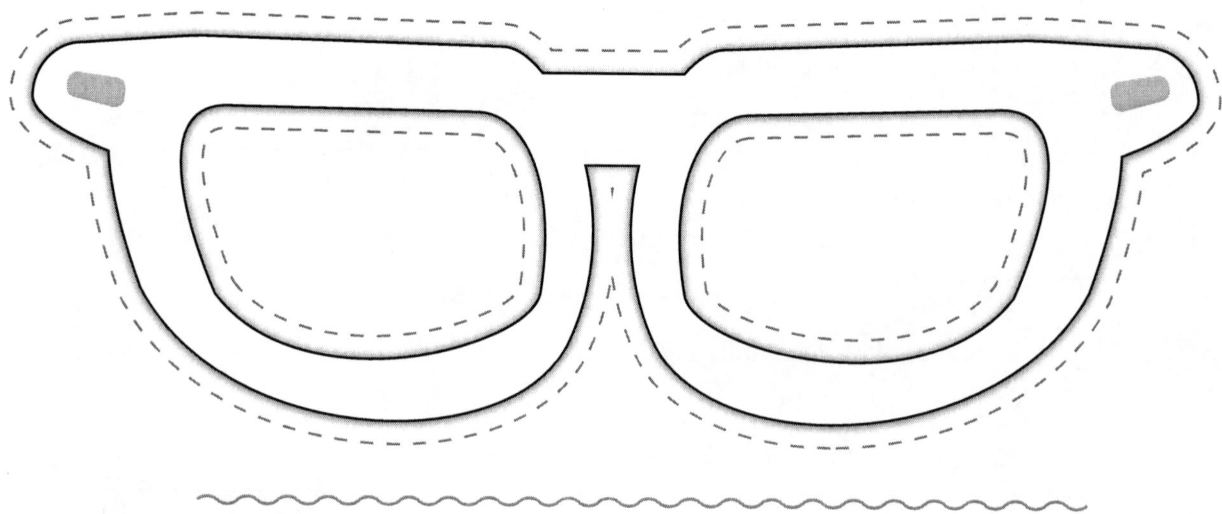

Magnifying Glass

Directions: Decorate the magnifying glass. Then, cut it out and use it as you closely read text.

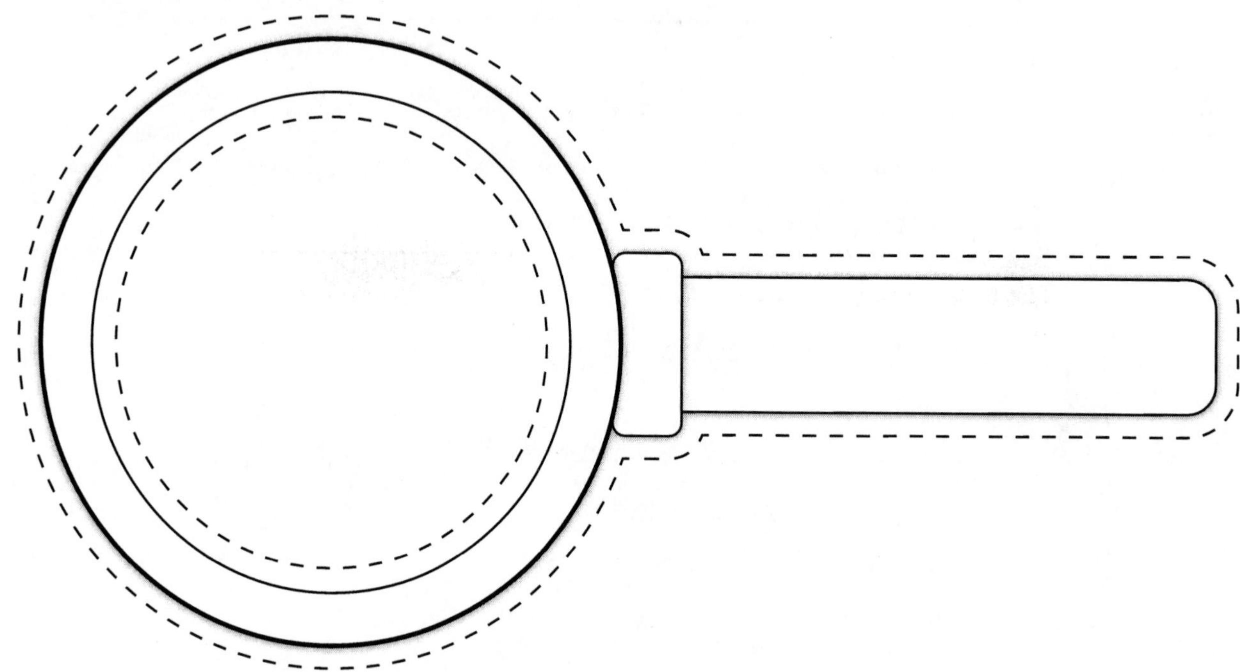

Close Reading Bookmarks

Ready, Set, Predict!

- Look over the text.
- Predict.
- Talk to a friend.

Go!

- Read.
- Mark words you like.

Reread to Clarify

- Read it again.
- Mark words.
- Talk to a partner.

Reread to Question

- Read it again.
- Ask questions.
- Talk to a partner.

Reread to Summarize and Respond

- Read it again.
- Summarize.
- Talk to a partner.

Ready, Set, Predict!

- Look over the text.
- Predict.
- Talk to a friend.

Go!

- Read.
- Mark words you like.

Reread to Clarify

- Read it again.
- Mark words.
- Talk to a partner.

Reread to Question

- Read it again.
- Ask questions.
- Talk to a partner.

Reread to Summarize and Respond

- Read it again.
- Summarize.
- Talk to a partner.

The Read It Again Song

Lyrics by Lori Oczkus

(Sung to the tune of "Frère Jacques")

Skim the text first,
Skim the text first.
Look for clues,
Look for clues.
Think about the topic
And the author's purpose.
Prediction,
Prediction.

Read the text now,
Read the text now,
Look for tricky words!
Look for tricky words!
Chop them into parts and
Think about what makes sense.
Clarify,
Clarify.

Read it again,
Read it again.
Question time,
Question time.
This time ask some questions:
Who, what, when, where, why, how?
Evidence,
Evidence.

Read it once more,
Read it once more.
What'd you learn?
What'd you learn?
Find the main ideas and
Share important details.
Summarize,
Summarize.